WARHOLCAPOTE

A NON-FICTION INVENTION

FROM THE WORDS OF

TRUMAN CAPOTE AND ANDY WARHOL

ADAPTED BY

ROB ROTH

SIMON & SCHUSTER

NEW YORK LONDON TORONTO SYDNEY NEW DELHI

Simon & Schuster
1230 Avenue of the Americas
New York, NY 10020

First Simon & Schuster hardcover edition September 2022

SIMON & SCHUSTER and colophon are registered trademarks of Simon & Schuster, Inc.

For information about special discounts for bulk purchases, please contact
Simon & Schuster Special Sales at 1-866-506-1949 or business@simonandschuster.com.

The Simon & Schuster Speakers Bureau can bring authors to your live event.
For more information or to book an event, contact the Simon & Schuster
Speakers Bureau at 1-866-248-3049 or visit our website at www.simonspeakers.com.

Manufactured in China

1 3 5 7 9 10 8 6 4 2

Library of Congress Cataloging-in-Publication Data is available.

ISBN 978-1-9821-0382-8
ISBN 978-1-9821-0384-2 (ebook)

For my parents,
who have made me the luckiest
"black-market baby" on Earth

CONTENTS

PREFACE

BLAKE GOPNIK

her eyes, squinty and bright green . . .
voice—boy husky
pencil-thin, bony kneed legs

and

fiery dutchboy hair
joel height
worn brown shorts and a yellow polo shirt

Those are a few lines from a whole sheet of notes that an art student named Andrew Warhola wrote, in a knock-kneed cursive he'd just invented, about the characters in a new novel he'd just read called *Other Voices, Other Rooms*. A twenty-three-year-old Truman Capote had published it early in 1948, seeing it received with both acclaim and disgust—but always with surprise.

PREFACE

The *New York Times* said Capote was "fascinated by decadence and . . . evil, or perhaps only by weakness. . . ." and that his book was "filled with sibilant whispering," hinting broadly at its homosexual themes.

Andy Warhol's notes on Capote's novel mark the first intersection between two of the most daringly gay creators in postwar America.

Rob Roth's *WARHOLCAPOTE*, based on words actually spoken by the two men, is set in the 1970s and '80s, toward the end of their close connection and not too long before their untimely deaths. But the very special, complex friendship captured by Roth had its roots in where they both came from.

When Capote's book appeared, Warhol was all of nineteen, a junior in college in his native Pittsburgh. He was also just coming out as gay, in a city whose judges soon declared homosexuals to be "society's greatest menace" and then tasked a police "morals" squad with eliminating it. (Two gay men were shot within weeks of the squad's creation; hundreds of others were soon arrested or blackmailed by the cops.)

How could Warhol not have been floored by a book that was about as openly queer as any writing of its era could be? Its thirteen-year-old hero, Joel Knox, gets described by Capote as defying mainstream notions "of what a 'real' boy should look like . . . He was too pretty, too delicate and fair-skinned; each of his features was shaped with a sensitive accuracy, and a girlish tenderness softened his eyes." He could have been talking about Warhol at that age. "Go on home and cut out paper dolls, sissy-britches," says a playmate to Joel. That's just what Warhol had done when a childhood strep infection had left him bedridden with spasms for three summers running.

One pan described the book as "lavender eyewash" and said it was evidence of the disintegration of American culture. For Warhol and certain others, the wounds that such words meant to inflict on Capote came with as much glory as shame: They were the stigmata of that moment in gay culture. Like all such markers of martyrdom, they stand as a sign of some kind of victory over your tormentors.

A contemporary of Warhol and Capote's remembered how, surrounded in college by "truculent" veterans on the G.I. Bill, the campus aesthetes found each other through Capote's new book: "To walk with Capote in your grasp was as distinctive, and as dissenting from the world's values, as a monk's habit."*

* Cynthia Ozick, quoted in Neil Printz, "Other Voices, Other Rooms: Between Andy Warhol and Truman Capote, 1948–1961" (PhD, New York University, 2000), 140.

PREFACE

In the twenty-first century, it is almost impossible to fully understand what it meant to be gay in postwar America, when both Warhol and Capote came of age, and came out. Two years after *Other Voices* appeared, the US Senate produced a report called *Employment of Homosexuals and Other Sex Perverts in Government* that included, among its other lies and brutalities, the assertion that "one homosexual can pollute a Government office." The Lavender Scare that followed stole the livelihoods of countless gay Americans. And yet Warhol and Capote dared to build their creative personas, and many of their creations, around limp wrists and levitating loafers.

In an amazing watershed for queer culture, Gore Vidal published a novel of gay life just a week before Capote's, and it was even more clearly and polemically "out." But with prose as spare and "muscular" as any straight author's, the novel comes closer to arguing for the potential normalcy of gay life—for its strong wrists and sensible shoes—than for the virtues of its exceptional culture. Warhol and Capote were almost unique in accepting, and in helping to create, a gay culture and art that could be proudly *other*. You can feel that in almost every word they utter in Roth's play; you can also feel how hard-won that acceptance was, even for the two men who did the accepting.

Eighteen months after the appearance of *Other Voices* Warhol moved to Capote's New York, where his interest in the writer turned into proper obsession.

"I started getting these letters from somebody who called himself Andy Warhol. They were, you know, fan letters," Capote recalled. "But not answering these Warhol letters didn't seem to faze him at all. I became Andy's Shirley Temple. After a while I began getting letters from him every day!" That pretty much squares with all kinds of records that document Warhol's crush. Capote's agent wrote to the young artist asking him to stop with the notes but was clearly more amused than distressed by his antics: "[Capote] said he'd been receiving some inane notes from one Warhol and thinks you must be slightly insane. So of course I told him you were."

For all his annoyance, Capote must have taken a certain pride in having a stalker of his very own, and one who was more than a bit above average, culture-wise. By the summer of 1952, Warhol had already scored his first New York solo show, in a velvet-draped gallery famous for its daring modernism—and for the camp antics of its owner, a former ballet dancer. The exhibition was called *Fifteen Drawings Based on the Writings of Truman Capote*, and Capote himself was impressed enough by its images to imagine them illustrating new editions of *Other Voices*.

PREFACE

For most of the 1950s, Warhol and Capote orbited each other at some slight distance—they could be seen dining at the gay-owned and decidedly camp Café Nicholson, if not at the same table then in the same dining room.

The duo got closer in the fall of 1966. That's when Capote celebrated the success of his blockbuster true-crime novel, *In Cold Blood*, with a masked ball at the Plaza Hotel, at which Warhol was among the celebrity guests. In the years that had passed since the two men's first encounters, their status had evened out. If Capote was an undoubted literary star, Warhol had at least equal status in the art world, and beyond, as the madcap capo of New York's underground scene. But where Warhol's fame had liberated him to make art that capitalized on his avowedly gay persona—the film *Blow Job* was one of his most (in)famous works of that era—the quite "straight" narrative of *In Cold Blood* followed Vidal's lead in divorcing Capote's writing from his persona, which continued to revel in queerness. You have to wonder if the creative gap between *Other Voices* and *In Cold Blood* helped stymie Capote's further growth as an artist—he achieved very little afterward, while Warhol's output never flagged.

In 1972, Warhol and Capote at last became true friends, after they were brought together by Capote's pal Lee Radziwill, Jackie Kennedy's sibling and thus a former

"First Sister of the United States." She was renting the lavish compound that Warhol's artistic success had allowed him to buy out on the tip of Long Island, where Capote also liked to summer. Before long, Warhol was suggesting to his new friend that the two do some kind of "sisters act."

Although it doesn't seem that Capote and Warhol ever had a romance, they went on to function like a classic pair of gay exes—loving but often catty as well, full of knowledge, but also reservations, about each other's past and behavior. That's the couple that is so perfectly captured in Roth's play.

It does seem to reveal a reversal, however, of the roles they'd played in 1948. We come to see Warhol as the model for some kind of successful integration into the wider culture. Capote seems more at sea.

That could be because Warhol, unlike Capote, had found a way to reconcile who he was and what he made. He had used the automatic outsider status he had always had as a gay man to power the most avant-garde art he could imagine, which by definition had to be far out of the mainstream. Even when he seemed to be courting the center, he was almost always busy working the margins. Capote, on the other hand, had never managed that kind of reconciliation. His most successful creations—not so much *Other Voices* as *Breakfast at Tiffany's* and *In Cold Blood*—spoke directly and easily to a mass audience and were meant to.

PREFACE

In Roth's true-life play—a parallel, in some ways, to Capote's true-crime novel—you get the sense that Capote is frustrated by conflicting desires: to be truly accepted deep into the mainstream while also preserving his gay outsiderism. But that didn't become an option in American culture until well after he'd been felled by the drugs and booze that his terminal angst forced on him. Whereas Roth's Warhol comes across as having a certain emotional ease that actually foreshadowed—because it helped cause—the hard-won ease of gay culture in the twenty-first century.

"I just assume everything is going to turn out for the worst and if it doesn't that's just so much gravy," Capote says to Warhol toward the middle of the play. "I mean, my life is so beleaguered and your life is so un-beleaguered."

And then, at its end: "When God does give one a gift, whatever it may be, composing or writing, for whatever pleasure it may bring, it also is a very painful thing to live with. It's a very excruciating life."

—May 2022

WARHOLCAPOTE

A NON-FICTION INVENTION

Dedicated to

RICK PAPPAS

for believing in this project from its inception . . .
and staying the course with me

and

PATRICK MEADE

for your loving heart, giant brain . . .
and all-around excellent husbanding

A NOTE ON THE PLAY

In 1978 Andy Warhol and Truman Capote decided to write a Broadway play.

Andy suggested that he tape-record their conversations with his Sony Walkman, and that the tapes would form the basis of the play. Truman enthusiastically agreed, and they began their collaboration.

The project was never completed, and the tapes, along with approximately three thousand others, were stored away. Upon Andy's death in 1987 the entire collection of cassette recordings was sent to the Warhol Museum in Pittsburgh, where they remained unlistened to, uncatalogued, and untranscribed.

In 2007, after lengthy discussion with The Andy Warhol Foundation and The Truman Capote Literary Trust, I was given permission to search for these recordings. Matt Wrbican, head archivist at the Warhol Museum, hunted through the cassettes, eventually unearthing fifty-nine

A NOTE ON THE PLAY

ninety-minute cassettes with "Truman" written on them. Approximately eighty hours of recordings. The majority of the tapes were undated.

The cassettes were digitally transferred and then transcribed word for word by a bonded court reporting company. The resulting transcripts are the source for the majority of the play. Direct quotes from Andy and Truman found in interviews and other recordings were employed as well.

The structure and location of the five conversations that form the play are wholly imagined. Every single word is directly from the mouths of Andy and Truman. A nonfiction invention.

I have followed the creative path Andy and Truman discussed together, which Andy, luckily, recorded.

—Rob Roth
New York City
October 22, 2020

PRODUCTION THOUGHTS

I believe that a simple production of the play works best.

For Michael Mayer's production at A.R.T., he guided the design team to a simple and elegant unit set, with a rear projection screen. In the play I have indicated "video transitions" between the scenes. Designer Darrel Maloney created graphic and moving images that were fairly abstract.

For the actors, the key here isn't to create an impersonation of Andy and Truman, but rather to reveal their true emotions and friendship.

The play is performed without an intermission.

The world premiere of

WARHOLCAPOTE

A NON-FICTION INVENTION

was produced by

the American Repertory Theater at Harvard University

DIANE PAULUS   DIANE QUINN   DIANE BORGER
Artistic Director   Executive Director   Producer

First Performance at the Loeb Drama Center
on September 10, 2017

THE CAST

(in order of appearance)

Andy Warhol . . . . Stephen Spinella

Truman Capote . . . . Dan Butler

THE CREATIVE TEAM

Director . . . . Michael Mayer

Scenic Design . . . . Stanley A. Meyer

Costume Design. . . . . Clint Ramos

Lighting Design. . . . . Kevin Adams

Sound Design . . . . John Gromada

Projections Design . . . . Darrel Maloney

Hair Design . . . . Charles G. LaPointe

Makeup Design . . . . Cookie Jordan

Dialect Coach . . . . Erika Bailey

Associate Director . . . . Johanna McKeon

Casting . . . . Jim Carnahan, CSA

Production Stage Manager . . . . Rick Steiger

By Special Arrangement with

The Truman Capote Literary Trust

and

The Andy Warhol Foundation for the Visual Arts, Inc.

(A pool of light comes up revealing ANDY
WARHOL. HE wears blue jeans, paint-covered
shoes, a button-down shirt and a silver wig.
HE gazes at the audience for a moment. Then
speaks directly to them:)

ANDY
Some people are peculiar.

My tape recorder and I have been married for
ten years now. My wife. When I say "we," I mean
my tape recorder and me. A lot of people don't
understand that. They're always putting it down
as an invasion of privacy, but I think everyone
should be bugged all the time. Bugged and
photographed.

Some people spend their whole lives thinking
about one particular famous person. They pick one
person who's famous, and they dwell on him or her.
They devote almost their entire consciousness to
thinking about this person they've never even
met. I admire people who do well with words, and
I thought Truman Capote filled up space with words
so well that when I first got to New York I began
writing short fan letters to him. If you ask any
famous person you'll find that almost every one of
them has at least one person who's obsessed with
them.

3

(The lights fade on ANDY as a pool of light
comes up on the other side of the stage
revealing TRUMAN CAPOTE. HE speaks directly
to the audience:)

TRUMAN
Andy Warhol had this obsession about me. I always
attracted a lot of attention, because, well
really, there isn't anybody else like me. In the
50's I started getting these letters from somebody
who called himself Andy Warhol. They were, you
know, fan letters. I never answer fan letters.
After a while I began getting letters from him
every day.

ANDY
I used to write Truman every day. For years. I
wanted to illustrate his short stories so badly.
I could almost picture Truman tilting his head
and arranging his words around the paper, making
them go together in a magical way that put you in
a certain mood when you read them. Truman was a
magic person.

TRUMAN
He wanted to become a friend of mine, wanted to
speak to me, to talk to me. He used to stand
outside my house, just stand there all day waiting
for me to come out. Somehow or other my mother
spoke to Andy out there on the street and she
invited him upstairs to the apartment. So, I sat
down and talked to him. He told me all about
himself, and how he lived some place with his

4

mother and twenty-five cats. He seemed a very shy, pale person. One of those hopeless people that you just know nothing's ever going to happen to. Just a hopeless, born loser.

                        ANDY
I called him on the phone every day. He was always so sweet. He always asked me how I was.

                        TRUMAN
He started calling me every day! He nearly drove me crazy. Then one day my mother told him not to call anymore. She was drunk at the time. So suddenly he stopped writing or calling me. Then, years later, I ran into him at Studio 54.

                        ANDY
Studio 54 is the best thing that's happened to New York City. Sometimes, when it's really fun, I can't help but think somebody will be murdered there. Every time I go I'm afraid I won't get in -- maybe they'll be somebody new at the door who won't recognize me. I always go with Halston, or in Halston.

                        TRUMAN
When I had known him in his previous incarnation, he seemed to me the loneliest, most friendless person I'd ever seen in my life. At 54 he was surrounded by seven or eight people, a real little entourage around this person I had really thought quite pitiable.

ANDY

At 54, Truman goes up into the crow's nest up
above the dance floor, and it's like his private
office. People come up to say hi, and he stays
until eight o'clock in the morning.

Cab to Studio 54 was three dollars and fifty cents.

(The lights change. A muffled disco beat plays
as a title appears:)

FROWARD

(The Crow's Nest at Studio 54. TRUMAN is
enjoying a cocktail and looking down onto the
crowded dance floor. ANDY enters and watches
for a few seconds, unnoticed, then:)

                    ANDY
Hi.

                    TRUMAN
Hello Andrew. How are you? Everything fine?

                    ANDY
Everybody looks like they're Somebody here.
Everyone looks so important.

                    TRUMAN
Yes. Love your shoes.

                    ANDY
Oh. They're painted.

                    TRUMAN
What?

                    ANDY
They're painted.

TRUMAN

Oh, really.

ANDY

Well, I was wearing boots for, you know, six
months and I was getting all these blisters.

TRUMAN

You probably don't remember, but I think I told
you to not wear boots.

ANDY

Oh, I know.

TRUMAN

Because they weren't good for you and they didn't
look right.

ANDY

Well, I'm back to shoes. Gee. The disco tonight is
as good as it was years ago.

TRUMAN

It is very good.

ANDY

Good-looking people and straight-looking people.
The busboys are all so young looking now. They're
all so nice.

TRUMAN

Very good-looking people, very amusing.

8

                    ANDY
Yeah. Not -- not too gay. It's just great. It
really is. This is so fun!

                   TRUMAN
I don't know why we don't open a nightclub.

                    ANDY
We'd be good at that.

                   TRUMAN
We should open the all-time great disco.

                    ANDY
I want to do that. It would be great.

                   TRUMAN
And we'd feed everything into it. And we'd make a
lot of money.

                    ANDY
I mean, the idea of just being there is fun. Let's
call it something. What can we call it?

                   TRUMAN
Hhmmm. Oh, Strange Dents.

                    ANDY
Strange Dents. Yeah!

                   TRUMAN
Strange Dents. That's my favorite name for it.

                      9

                              ANDY
Dents. Strange Dents.

                             TRUMAN
Strange Dents. D-E-N-T-S. Strange Dents.

                              ANDY
This is fun. God.

                             TRUMAN
We'll make millions!

                              ANDY
Millions! Truman, have you ever been taped before?

                             TRUMAN
Sure. The thing I like to do most in the whole
world is talk!

        (ANDY takes out his Sony Recorder and places
        it between them. We can see the little red
        record light is already on.)

If I had to choose between writing and talking --
well, I just don't know what I'd do! You know just
the other day I was going through the dictionary,
and I found the perfect word for you. It describes
you perfectly.

                              ANDY
Oh. Really? What's the word?

                               10

                    TRUMAN
It's called "froward." F-R-O-W-A-R-D.

                    ANDY
What's it mean?

                    TRUMAN
Froward is a very marvelous word. It means
somebody who's very original and very perverse and
contrariwise. Something that just doesn't actually
fit. I'm froward and you're froward.

                    ANDY
Oh gee. That sounds great. It's a good title for a
book.

                    TRUMAN
And nobody ever uses froward.

    (Pause.)

Whatever happened to Liza?

                    ANDY
Liza? I think she's starting with Scorsese.

                    TRUMAN
Well, he's a big nothing anyway.

                    ANDY
Martin? Oh, no, no. He's actually pretty good.

                       11

                    TRUMAN
You like him?

                      ANDY
Yeah, I do. Yeah.

                    TRUMAN
I think he's sweet and nice, but that movie he
made with Robert De Niro and Liza has got to be
one of the all-time worst films ever.

                      ANDY
It had good music and she was good.

                    TRUMAN
You didn't think that was -- you thought that was
good?

                      ANDY
No. No, I didn't like it. I just like her singing,
you know, it's just, she's good.

                    TRUMAN
Oh, well, Liza's got something, but, you know --
and I love her. She's a really good girl. And her
mother was one of my greatest friends. You know,
I knew Liza when she was eight or nine years old.
Liza really actually has talent.

                      ANDY
Halston told me lots of gossip. He said that the
night before, when the doorbell rang, it was
Liza. Her life's very complicated now. Like she

was walking down the street with Jack Haley, her husband, and they'd run into Marty who she's having an affair with, and Marty confronted her that she was having an affair with Baryshnikov, and Marty said how could she. This was going on with her husband, standing there! Halston said it was all true, and he also said that Jack Haley wasn't gay. I was right! I didn't think so. So when the doorbell rang the night before it was Liza, in a hat pulled down so nobody would recognize her, and she said to Halston, "give me every drug you've got."

                    TRUMAN
Oh Liza! She's wild!

                    ANDY
She's so fun. Oh! I went to Madison Square Garden to see Elton John. He was sensational. And oh God, is he fat. He had on a silver lamé caftan, but tight -- a skintight caftan -- and the audience loved him.

                    TRUMAN
I went to a David Bowie concert and it wasn't very special.

                    ANDY
David Bowie never really made that much money.

                    TRUMAN
You know, we could have all flown out to the Rolling Stones concert in LA last night.

ANDY

You mean the night before? Really?

TRUMAN

Yes, there was this private plane going out and I
started to call you up. Just for the evening and
the concert, and then we would fly back.

(The lights change. ANDY speaks HIS thoughts
aloud to the audience:)

ANDY

*When you're really really involved with something
you're usually thinking about something else.*

(The lights restore.)

TRUMAN

One thing I'll say about Mick Jagger. He's
fascinating in the sense that he's one of the
most total actors that I've ever seen. He has
this remarkable quality of being absolutely able
to be totally extroverted. Very few people can
be entirely, absolutely, altogether extroverted.
It's a rare, delicate, strange thing. Just to
pull yourself and out go -- WHAMM! This he can do
to a remarkable degree. Mick's an extraordinary
performer.

(The lights change. ANDY's thoughts:)

ANDY

I'll get three full-sided tapes out of this!

(The lights restore.)

TRUMAN

But what I think's amazing about him is that
there's no single thing of all the things he does
that he's really good at. He really can't dance,
and in fact, he really can't move. He's moving in
the most awkward kind of curious parody between
an American majorette girl and Fred Astaire. But
somehow the combination works.

ANDY

Did you like traveling around with them?

TRUMAN

Oh I enjoyed it. I just didn't want to write about
it because it didn't interest me creatively. But
I enjoyed it as an experience. I thought it was
amusing.

ANDY

What was the problem with writing the article?

TRUMAN

There has to be some element of mystery to me
about it. Something that I can't imagine. That was
my problem. Since there was nothing to "find out,"
I just couldn't be bothered writing it. Does that
make sense to you?

ANDY

Yes.

15

TRUMAN

To me, every act of art is the act of solving a
mystery.

ANDY

But it seems like there's just so much material on
that trip . . .

TRUMAN

Yes there's material, but it's just that,
material. It doesn't have an echo. You know?

ANDY

Gee. Yeah.

(Pause.)

Truman, we should work together.

TRUMAN

Really!

ANDY

Let's write a new play. We've got to do eight
plays on Broadway all running at the same time.
Fast plays.

TRUMAN

Oh yes. Broadway! Everybody always says it's dead,
it's gone -- but it always comes back. Theaters
last year made more money than ever.

ANDY

Gee Truman, can't I just tape you? You know,
the real thing, and do plays about real people.
Actually, if we just tape it.

TRUMAN

See, that's the kind of thing I want to do.
Reality and art intertwined to the point that
there is no identifiable area of demarcation.

ANDY

And then what do we really talk about?

TRUMAN

I mean, it will be like a small play in which you
see everything about a person. Every word of it
true. Let's make this some absolutely fantastic
thing.

ANDY

I don't think plot is important. If you see two
people talking, you can watch it over and over
again without being bored -- you get involved --
you miss things -- you come back to it -- you see
new things. But you can't see the same thing over
again if it has a plot because you already know
the ending.

TRUMAN

It all has to do basically with truth treated in a
fictional form. To see a certain reality about what
people are thinking. To see what is going on in
their heads and everything.

                    ANDY
I think it should be a situation comedy.

                    TRUMAN
No. I know exactly what it should be and I want
you to be serious about it.

                    ANDY
Okay. Why can't it be a situation comedy?

                    TRUMAN
Because it can't be.

                    ANDY
Oh.

                    TRUMAN
Because it's going to be a success.

                    ANDY
Oh. Okay.

                    TRUMAN
It's going to be something that's going to run for
a long time.

                    ANDY
Oh.

                    TRUMAN
And be a national institution!

ANDY

Really!? God.

    (The lights change. Video transition. A title
    appears:)

DISEQUILIBRIUM

ANDY
Cab to La Petite Marmite, on 49th in the Beekman
Towers -- three dollars and fifty cents.

(ANDY and TRUMAN seated at a secluded table
in La Petite Marmite restaurant. They toast
one another:)

TRUMAN
Two living legends.

ANDY
I thought we were two dead legends.

TRUMAN
They should put up a monument to us. We're two
living legends. And by God, we're the only two.

ANDY
How about two legends really get drunk . . .

TRUMAN
Drunk and disorderly.

ANDY
God.

                         TRUMAN
You see. I was right to do it.

                          ANDY
Oh. Look at you. Oh, yeah. It's just -- yeah.

                         TRUMAN
Remember, you all told me not to do it. Do you
remember standing there and telling me you don't
need it?

                          ANDY
Oh, yeah.

                         TRUMAN
Don't do it. Don't do it.

                          ANDY
It looks good. Yeah, it looks great.

                         TRUMAN
And I said, I do need it. I'm going to look so
much better.

                          ANDY
You do. God. You look great. God. It's just
amazing how different you look. I can't believe it.
God.

                         TRUMAN
My skin looks real good. My skin is beautiful.
B-E-A-U-T-I-F-U-L!!

ANDY

We want to do a new picture of you.

TRUMAN

Well, when I'm all done. Changing -- finish the
hair and whatnot, then I'm going to look real
good. I knew you would be pleased when I finally
did it all.

ANDY

Yeah, it looks really terrific. And you're losing
so much weight, too. It's just incredible.

TRUMAN

Well, I'm going to get very, very, very thin. Very
thin.

ANDY

Oh.

TRUMAN

Even thin enough to please you.

ANDY

Do you know -- do you know who really looks great,
is C. Z. She lost a lot of weight.

TRUMAN

Yeah?

ANDY

Oh, yeah. I mean, she looks young again. Because
remember how heavy she was getting and stuff?

                    TRUMAN
Yeah. I've known C. Z. through all of her life.
There's one thing that she will admit. See, she
was a fat girl to begin with.

                    ANDY
Oh, really.

                    TRUMAN
She was a big, fat girl.

                    ANDY
Oh, really.

                    TRUMAN
She has these big, fat arms.

                    ANDY
Yeah.

                    TRUMAN
That's the one thing she can't get rid of.

                    ANDY
Oh, really. Oh.

                    TRUMAN
Because she's got these big, fat arms.

                    ANDY
Oh. Is that from riding or --

TRUMAN

No, no, no. That's something that -- people who were ever very fat have one area left on their body. No matter how thin they get, there's one part of them that stays fat. Did you know that Allan Carr had this bypass and he got down to about 200 pounds.

ANDY

Oh, I know. What a butterball. If you pushed him over he'd roll! I heard that he eats so much he actually, he faints. Can you believe it? It's scary.

TRUMAN

Well, I can — not only believe, but I also understand it. There are certain people who are compulsive drinkers. Certain people who are compulsive sex -- compulsive smokers, compulsive drinkers. . . . And with Allan, it's eating. I mean, it's a neurotic illness. He's very insecure. And he just keeps on eating and eating and eating. I know people that keep on drinking and drinking or keep on doing whatever the hell they're doing because they've got some great free-floating anxiety.

ANDY

He has a problem. I mean, I know he does, but I just can't believe it somehow because, you know, he is such a happy person. I mean, some people are peculiar.

                    TRUMAN
Allan gave a party for me in Hollywood, which was
one of the all-time, total nightmares I've ever --
I stayed for one hour and 15 minutes.

                    ANDY
You mean it wasn't a good party?

                    TRUMAN
Well, the whole thing was madness. Because you
walk in, everybody recognizes you. Everybody knows
you. They close in on you and --

                    ANDY
It's so hard. I know. It really is.

                    TRUMAN
Well, you can go to certain restaurants and things
and people don't bother you.

                    ANDY
You're more famous, so they won't bother me,
they'll bother you.

        (Laughter.)

                    TRUMAN
I'm going to tell you the best story of all time
about people bothering, because it's really,
really funny.

                    ANDY
Oh. Okay. Wow.

(ANDY moves the tape recorder closer to
TRUMAN.)

TRUMAN
I was in a bar in Key West with Tennessee
Williams. It was very, very crowded. So there was
this woman and her husband, they were sitting
about four or five tables away. And she came over
to me with one of those eyebrow things, those
things that they write things on the eyebrows.
And she said, I want you to autograph my navel.
I said, "oh, come on. Forget it." And Tennessee
said, "oh, for heaven's sakes. Go on, do it.
What the hell difference does it make?" So I very
carefully wrote, like a clockwork, my name right
around the navel with this eyebrow pencil. So she
went back to her table where she was with her
husband, who was absolutely bombed out of his
mind.

So he got up and came over and he unzipped his fly.
Pulled out his cock and handed me this eyebrow
pencil and he said, "since you're autographing
things, would you mind autographing this?"

And I said, "I don't know that I could actually
autograph it, but perhaps with some effort I could
initial it."

ANDY
Oh, that's great.

26

TRUMAN

It really brought down the maison. Those people
laughed for 15 minutes.

ANDY

Gee. That is funny.

TRUMAN

I'll be right back.

(TRUMAN takes his carry bag and exits.
ANDY is alone. Checks the tape recorder.
The lights change. ANDY's thoughts:)

ANDY

*The acquisition of my tape recorder really finished
whatever emotional life I might have had, but I was
glad to see it go. Nothing was ever a problem again,
because a problem just meant a good tape, and when a
problem transforms itself into a good tape it's not
a problem anymore. Everybody knew that and performed
for the tape. You couldn't tell which problems were
real and which problems were exaggerated. Better
yet, the people telling you the problems couldn't
decide anymore if they were really having the
problems or if they were just performing.*

(The lights restore. TRUMAN returns. HE is
agitated.)

TRUMAN

I've got to tell you something that I didn't tell
you.

27

ANDY

Oh God. You do?

TRUMAN

Did you see that piece about me in the *New York Times Magazine*? Did you read that -- well, you did. I mean, all of these people are making so much money out of writing nasty things about me. On the whole, I think in a certain way I've been the most attacked person continuously. I'm just writing about people that I know about, what happened. Well, you'd really think I killed Lindbergh's baby. And I didn't do nothing. I mean, I didn't do the slightest thing that any creative artist wouldn't have done -- I mean, and the way people have treated me about it, I mean, it's unbelievable. All a writer has is his own experience. I mean, that's all that a writer has to write about is what they see and hear and whatnot. If you happen to capture my imagination, for some reason, and I decide to write about you, and you don't like what I wrote about you, which is entirely possible, then yes, I'm a dangerous friend.

(The lights change. ANDY's thoughts:)

ANDY

Writers have to do things like that. I mean, that's the only way they know to write things down. They have to experience things.

(The lights restore.)

                    TRUMAN
I'm going to publish my book. *Answered Prayers* is
going to be a beautiful book. It's not anything
to do with malice or anything. It's a really very
beautiful book, very compassionate.

                    ANDY
It sounds so exciting. The *Esquire* chapters were
so great.

                    TRUMAN
You're really going to like that book.

                    ANDY
It sounds great.

                    TRUMAN
It's my life's work, that book.

                    ANDY
And the people you know are so interesting, to
combine them together.

                    TRUMAN
It's been incredible. Even people who are not
friends of mine, basically, like Tennessee, wrote
me a letter saying that they were just absolutely
shocked and amazed -- (searching through HIS carry
bag) -- Don't let me lose this thing . . . (pulls
out various prescription vials). Oh it's all so
insane and absurd (more vials, then finds the
letter). Well, here it is.

29

ANDY

Oh, Truman, why don't you read it in Tennessee's
voice?

TRUMAN

(Laughter.)

No.

ANDY

Oh, please, please, please you do Tennessee's
voice so great. Come on. Come on. Read it.

TRUMAN

No, no, no, I don't want to make fun of him
anymore. I only can do it when I'm making fun of
him.

ANDY

Read it in your own voice then. But read it in
Tennessee's voice.

TRUMAN

I can't.

ANDY

Yes, you can.

TRUMAN

"Dear Truman, knowing my history I feel sure
that you will receive this letter sincerely
well intended in every way. I am truly aghast

by the media's exploitation of your period of
disequilibrium." That's a new word for me. "I
have been through it all myself. Even when I was
temporarily outraged by that monster piece in
Esquire. I have admired, as I have always, your
brilliant artistry. In circumstances of this sort
I know from experience it is not pity we want, nor
expressions of it. It occurred to me, though, that
this might be an appropriate time to say to you
something that you said to me once. 'I care about
you more than you know.' I am deeply concerned
that you give to your being the care that your
talent deserves. Perhaps the thing most to help
you right now is your incomparable sense of humor.
It is hard for me to write in this vein, but rest
a bit and never, never stop laughing. With new
understanding, your old friend, Tennessee."

ANDY

God. It's so great. This is Tennessee. God.

TRUMAN

So, the *New York Times*. Okay. Well, but, I mean,
it's awful how those people just feed and live off
of you. I'm sick of those people. Because I really
wouldn't have minded particularly, but almost 50
percent of it was lies. I mean, absolute straight-
out, bona fide lies. Oh, it was dreadful.

ANDY

All interviews are preordained, Truman. They know
what they want to write about you and they know
what they think about you before they ever talk to

31

you, so they're just looking for words and details
from here and there to back up what they've
already decided they are going to say.

                    TRUMAN
I mean, it was one of the worst things I've
ever read. I think the only unforgivable sin is
deliberate cruelty. It's taken me a long time
to discover how much endurance I have for pain.
How much pain I can actually withstand, and
still function. And it was so incredibly ineptly
written. Hack, hack, hack.

                    ANDY
You know, you let -- you let it happen. You did
let it happen.

                    TRUMAN
I didn't let it happen.

                    ANDY
Yes, you did, Truman. I mean, you could stop it if
you wanted to. I mean, you let it happen.

                    TRUMAN
How could I have stopped it?

                    ANDY
Well, you talked to the girl. You gave her an
interview.

                    TRUMAN
I only talked to her twice.

ANDY

Well, that twice was too much. But I think --
after this article, I think -- You know, nobody's
ever written anything like this before. I mean,
they haven't. I think it would be great not to
be publicized too much. I think it's going to be
really scary to be publicized. I don't know. The
way things are going, it's just going to be really
terrible. People in the news are going to be the
people that people are going to really attack. I
mean, anybody, you know, in the news and stuff like
that. And it's going to be really awful, I think.
I hope it doesn't happen. It just seems like it
will. I don't know.

TRUMAN

I've just had enough. My whole life has just been
nothing but just -- what I don't need is to be
destructed all the time.

(The lights change. ANDY's thoughts:)

ANDY

*Some people let the same problem make them
miserable for years when they could just say, "So
what." "My mother didn't love me -- so what." "My
husband won't ball me -- so what." "I'm a success,
but I'm still alone -- so what." I don't know how
I made it through all the years before I learned
how to do that trick.*

(The lights restore.)

33

You get upset about those things, Truman. You
should . . .

TRUMAN

Jesus God, Andy. If I got upset about those
things, if I really got upset about it, I mean,
I'd be in Forest Lawn, but I just think about
it for a minute, and then I cast it away. For
Christ's sake, so would you be in Forest Lawn.

ANDY

You know the plot next to Marilyn in Forest Lawn
is available for $25,000.

TRUMAN

Let's buy it, and they can put us all together.

ANDY

We can be famous. We can share it. It will be 12
and a half, okay, and we can be cremated. You can
have one half section, okay?

TRUMAN

Marilyn Monroe was somebody I knew real well over
a 10-year period. And I was very, very fond of
Marilyn. But I really fixed old Marilyn once.

ANDY

Why? What did --

TRUMAN

Well, she was really awfully dependent on me at
a certain point in her life when she was in New

York. I really liked her a lot, we had lunch all
the time. Well, she was -- I always figured she
would be late, you know. But one day she was -- we
were supposed to meet at 1:15 and it was getting
to 2:00. And I just got up and I left. And I left
a little note for her and it said, "stop playing
Marilyn Monroe or else forget me. Yours truly,
T.C." And she calls me up she says, "I'm in floods
of tears." I says, "you don't sound like it."

(Laughter.)

                    ANDY
Wow.

                    TRUMAN
But of course, her thing of being late was just
completely neurotic. There are people who are just
neurotic about being late. I'm always on time.
Always exactly on the dot.

                    ANDY
Always.

(Pause. TRUMAN finishes HIS drink.)

                    TRUMAN
My doctor suggested that I adopt some healthier
hobby other than wine-tasting and fornication. So
I'm going to get all pulled together. You can come
out and visit me at the center.

ANDY

Okay, all right. I'll come out and visit you. That
would be really great. Oh, Truman, we're going to
miss you.

TRUMAN

And if luck allows and discipline holds, I will
have time to arrive at higher altitudes, where the
air is thin but the view exhilarating.

ANDY

It is one plane ride, and then you can take a car?

TRUMAN

Yes. It is not a big trip at all. I'm getting
ready to have a last sensational thirty years.

(Pause.)

Andy, would you call me up?

ANDY

Oh, sure, yeah.

TRUMAN

I mean, would you, really?

ANDY

Yeah.

TRUMAN

You see, I might call you, but I didn't think
you'd call me.

                    ANDY
Oh, yes, I would.

                    TRUMAN
You would?

                    ANDY
Yeah.

                    TRUMAN
I wondered.

    (Pause.)

    (The lights change. Video transition. A title
    appears:)

MARBLES

ANDY

Lunch at the studio with Truman. Ten dollars.

(ANDY's studio. TRUMAN is admiring ANDY's paintings.)

TRUMAN

I gasp at your energy.

ANDY

My heavens! Really? God.

TRUMAN

You're fantastic.

ANDY

Oh. Well --

TRUMAN

I think you're one of the all-time most fabulous people that I've ever known. I made a list of 15 people the other day.

ANDY

That you could send to the moon. Right?

TRUMAN

No. I made a list of people who I considered extraordinarily gifted. I didn't put it any other way, just extraordinarily gifted people in a worldwide way and why in one sentence. And you're in it.

ANDY

God. You know, blue's your color. You look so beautiful in blue.

TRUMAN

You always say nice things, Andy.

ANDY

So, Truman, are you going to piss on my paintings? You've got to. It's a work of art.

TRUMAN

All right. Well, I can pee in tubes. I'm sure I can pee on a painting.

ANDY

You peed in a tube? What do you mean you peed in a tube?

TRUMAN

Well, every time you go to the hospital they give you a tube and say "pee in the tube."

ANDY

Oh, God, Truman, we could have a double show. You know, the Truman Capote—Andy Warhol piss

paintings. Do you want to, Truman? You have to
drink a lot of beer.

TRUMAN
I drink an enormous amount of Tab.

ANDY
I mean, you can give up writing and become an
artist. Right?

TRUMAN
Well, you gave up art and became a writer.

ANDY
I really think you could have a machine that
paints all day long for you and do it really well,
and you could do something else instead, and you
could turn out really wonderful canvases. It would
be different if some machine did it.

TRUMAN
Extraordinary.

(The lights change. ANDY's thoughts:)

ANDY
*Truman is just in such good spirits. I mean, does
he really have a problem? He looks like he feels
fine, but is he feeling fine?*

(The lights restore.)

So, how was it, being away? I tried calling you
there. I never could get through. No one would ever
answer. Are you planning to go back at all or --

                    TRUMAN
Go back? There?

                    ANDY
Yeah.

                    TRUMAN
No.

                    ANDY
Oh great.

                    TRUMAN
I have, I mean, carte blanche to go back. I could
go there any time I wanted. But I don't really
want to do that.

                    ANDY
Oh. Okay.

                    TRUMAN
It was nice. I liked it. It was okay. It was a
lot of work -- because, I mean, you know, it's
a really rigorous program. It's a very serious
place. I mean, they don't play games. I mean, it's
not Silver Hill. It's very comfortable. They have
a very good staff. They have 290 people on the
staff.

                    ANDY
Did you meet anybody interesting there?

                    TRUMAN
Lots of interesting.

                    ANDY
Really?

                    TRUMAN
Some of them I liked very much. Very talented and
very -- from all over the world.

                    ANDY
Really. Oh. Any really fascinating people or . . .

                    TRUMAN
Yes, quite a few.

                    ANDY
Were you the most interesting person there?

                    TRUMAN
I was the most famous. I don't know that I was the
most interesting. There's a big difference.

                    ANDY
But you must have been very different.

                    TRUMAN
I was in an extremely difficult position because
everybody that ran the place was making a great
point via I wasn't, quote, anybody. On the other

                    42

hand, I mean, I was the biggest thing that ever happened to them.

                    ANDY
You should have worn a wig. Have you ever seen Jackie with a wig on somewhere else looking different? I mean, do you think she would ever do it?

                    TRUMAN
No. But I've always said that Jackie Kennedy was the world's greatest female impersonator.

                    ANDY
No. But do you think she's ever done that? I mean. You know, like put on a red wig or something like that. To hide, I mean -- It would be fun if she did. It would be really, really fun. I think she must be a fun person.

                    TRUMAN
Who?

                    ANDY
Jackie.

                    TRUMAN
She's not fun at all.

                    ANDY
She's not fun at all? Really?

                    TRUMAN
Jackie Kennedy? Fun?

43

ANDY

Yeah. But maybe just during -- what period?

TRUMAN

I've spent an awful lot of time with her. And
if that's your idea of fun. . . . I knew Jackie
before she was even married to him.

ANDY

And she wasn't fun then either?

TRUMAN

She was never fun. When I first met Jackie I thought
she was very bright, charming, well read. We used
to see a lot of each other. And then, after she
married Jack and went to the White House she seemed
to survive by sheer publicity alone. She just
developed this peculiar star quality. It happens
to people. You never know quite what it is. It's
like this candle has been lighted inside them.
They never again quite look like anybody else.
And then, too, it all made Jackie quite cynical
where she hadn't been before. By the time of the
assassination she had become a personality in her
own right. And after, that became quite a cross to
bear. I mean it was really awful, because she was
hounded and hounded. Jackie said to me once, "Oh,
let's face it. I'm just a freak! Because of an
accident of history, I'll always be an object of
curiosity, like something you go to see in a freak
show." And I said, "Jackie, don't you think that's
a very hard way of looking at it?" And she said,
"It may be hard, but it's true."

44

                    ANDY
Are you serious? I can't believe it.

                    TRUMAN
It's true.

                    ANDY
I am not bothered about any of the things that
are written about me: I just look at the pictures
in the articles, it doesn't matter what they say
about me, I just read the textures of the words.
And if you look at something long enough, I've
discovered, the meaning goes away. I'm going to
get the Polaroid together. I want to do a portrait
Truman.

        (ANDY exits to get the Polaroid camera.)

                    TRUMAN
Oh, great. That's terrific.

                    ANDY
How do you want your portrait done? With that
outfit?

                    TRUMAN
Great! This is going to be fun!

        (ANDY begins shooting pictures and places
        the developing photos into HIS jacket pocket.
        ANDY encourages TRUMAN as HE shoots.)

ANDY

Good. That's great. So, did you meet anybody nice
up there?

TRUMAN

The only person that I really really liked while
I was there died. Because he had cirrhosis of the
liver.

ANDY

Oh. That's nice.

TRUMAN

And he was in good condition really, except for
this one thing.

ANDY

Did you ever have a bad liver, Truman?

TRUMAN

Nope.

ANDY

Never?

TRUMAN

Never.

ANDY

Oh, good.

                    TRUMAN
Despite everything I did to myself --
everything -- I just came out as one of the
world's number one healthy people.

                    ANDY
Really? Great.

                    TRUMAN
It's really extraordinary when you consider what I
did to myself. But at least I learned one thing,
and that is that I want to live, that I do believe
in life, that I do have something to say about
life. When I thought I was going to die, and I did
for a while, I wept -- not for myself but for the
stories I knew, the poetry that belonged to me.

                    ANDY
Can we do one more roll?

                    TRUMAN
Okay.

        (ANDY puts a new cartridge into the camera
        and continues shooting as THEY talk.)

                    ANDY
Is there enough good material to work up -- in
Minnesota?

                    TRUMAN
Don't let me commence.

ANDY

I mean, can you write something from there? I
mean, anything interesting?

TRUMAN

I could write an eight-volume thing from my mind.

ANDY

Oh, really. Was it fascinating? Really interesting
things happening? Now, you stay there and I'll
move around, because I just want to get a different
part of you.

TRUMAN

Sometime, some night, I'll sit and talk to you
about my life in Hazelden.

ANDY

Really?

TRUMAN

At the moment, I mean, I'm up to here with it and
can't start. But at some point it is going to
all come out, but I had that place really turned
upside down.

ANDY

Oh. You did?

TRUMAN

They didn't want me to go. Up to the very last
minute -- I mean, I'm not kidding when I say they were
trying to take my luggage out of the station wagon.

                    ANDY
Oh, really. Why?

                    TRUMAN
I was the most interesting thing that had ever
happened to them in the history of Hazelden.

                    ANDY
Yeah, just a little more three-quarter.

                    TRUMAN
And I don't say that with any vanity --

                    ANDY
Three-quarter.

                    TRUMAN
I know -- because in many ways it ruined the point
of ever going to Hazelden.

                    ANDY
That's better. It must be hard to go anywhere like
that. I mean, when you do become --

                    TRUMAN
The whole point is to make you feel as though
you're just absolutely no different from anybody.

                    ANDY
That's good, yeah.

                    49

                    TRUMAN

They begin by grinding you down in a very special
way, you know.

                     ANDY

What do they do to you? Just talk to you or --

                    TRUMAN

You see you're doing these things they're -- they
call it the 12 Steps.

                     ANDY

Very good. Look this way now.

                    TRUMAN

I mean, they right away see 12 steps for you -- they
see these 12 steps and they begin to follow it, and
like this: one, two, three, four, five, six --

                     ANDY

Make it three-quarter. That's good.

                    TRUMAN

 -- and it becomes, you know, like -- like
Catholicism. It is a religion. And the people who
are really deep into it really think of it and
accept it as a religion.

                     ANDY

Come look.

          (TRUMAN joins ANDY. THEY look at the
          photos.)

These are too light. I always try to make them
light, because we make the screen --

                    TRUMAN
You know, Andy, that really is the best.

                    ANDY
That's not the best. Here's the best one. This is
much better.

                    TRUMAN
That's very similar.

                    ANDY
This is the best. This is the best one.

                    TRUMAN
Here's three that I like. One, two, three.

                    ANDY
Photography is a funny thing, isn't it? My idea
of a good picture is one that's in focus and of a
famous person doing something unfamous.

                    TRUMAN
Oh, yeah. I only like those three pictures.

                    ANDY
Oh.

                    TRUMAN
Yeah, that one. This one, too. As a matter of
fact, I think almost all of them are good, one way
or another.

          (The lights change. ANDY's thoughts:)

                     ANDY
God. Truman is like a different person. So different.
He sounds sensible today and he hasn't had a drink.

          (The lights restore.)

                    TRUMAN
AA works for certain people. It works for them
perfectly. The more simple-minded you are, the
better it is. It's very difficult to be intelligent
and to go to AA.

                     ANDY
Oh, really.

                    TRUMAN
Certain people take -- once they basically start
taking a certain kind of drink or pill, they do it
in order to, quote/unquote, feel normal.

                     ANDY
Oh. It's true. I know.

                    TRUMAN
When they take a -- a couple of drinks, they feel the
way most people feel when they're feeling normal.

ANDY

But isn't it fantastic? People do think that they
know what normal is.

TRUMAN

Uh-huh.

ANDY

Isn't it fascinating? That's so great.

TRUMAN

Okay. This is the one thing about you that drives
me out of my mind. You always think everything's
great.

ANDY

It is. Isn't it? You don't think it is? Oh, you
have to think that way. It is.

TRUMAN

It's this -- this thing of yours, of having this
optimistic thing about people. It's this one thing
with you -- that you always say -- "oh, he's
wonderful." "Oh, she's great." You know why it
annoys me?

ANDY

Why?

TRUMAN

Because there are people that I hate. There are
people that I want to say to you, listen, Joe
Blow, I can't stand him. I hate him. I hate him

53

for the following reasons. I don't want you to
say to me, "oh, but he's really -- he's really a
rather nice guy." Why do you do that?

                    ANDY
Uh, I don't know. I usually like them.

                    TRUMAN
Well, it must be something real. I mean, it
must be that you really think that. I am never
generous. I am mean, mean, mean. I just assume
everything is going to turn out for the worst and
if it doesn't that's just so much gravy. I mean,
my God. I mean, my life is so beleaguered and your
life is so un-beleaguered. I mean, I know that
your life is beleaguered.

                    ANDY
Yeah. Some of my marbles are missing. Something is
missing . . . the marbles.

          (The lights change. Video transition. A title
          appears:)

15 MINUTES

ANDY
Cab to Elaine's. Three dollars and fifty cents.

(A quiet table at Elaine's. TRUMAN takes a very long swallow of HIS cocktail and puts the empty glass on the table.)

TRUMAN
When I think of the people that I've known, you know, oh.

ANDY
God. Yeah, I know. The people you know are so interesting.

TRUMAN
I mean, I just can't believe that these people could have been in my life. Bogie was a great friend of mine.

ANDY
Wow. God.

(ANDY once again moves the tape recorder closer to TRUMAN.)

                    TRUMAN

This is an amusing story. I really wanted to go to
bed with Bogie.

                    ANDY

Wanted Bogart? Ooh. This is while you were working
on that wonderful movie --

                    TRUMAN

Beat the Devil.

                    ANDY

Yeah.

                    TRUMAN

I was saving that fucking movie for them.

                    ANDY

That must have been so exciting.

                    TRUMAN

I mean, I just wanted to go to bed with him
just -- just in a kind of experimental way. And he
was very aware of this.

                    ANDY

Ooh.

                    TRUMAN

This was really funny. Bogie knew -- well, I
mean, everybody knew. Anyway, one night -- it got
kind of late and Bogie says, "I'm going to go
upstairs." And I said, "oh, I ought to go upstairs

with you and I'll have a drink." And I could see
he was getting a little nervous.

                    ANDY
Nervous.

                    TRUMAN
So we went up and it was -- it was still sort of
winter. It was very cold. I said, "why don't you
have a nice time, and I'll just sit here and talk
to you." And all the time I could see, you know,
there were two things going on. One was a kind of
alertiveness, and the other thing that was going
on was shall I or shan't I, you know.

          (The lights change. ANDY's thoughts:)

                    ANDY
Truman makes up so much. I mean, how could anybody
make it with Truman? God.

          (The lights restore.)

                    TRUMAN
I mean, you could see it. It was just like
something painted across somebody's eyes. So, I
said, "are you nice and warm in your bed? Wouldn't
you like me to get under there? Don't you think
we would be warmer?" He says, "no, no, no. I'm
perfectly all right." I said, "oh, Bogie. What are
you so frightened about? It's nothing to be so
frightened of. Do you mean to tell me that nobody
in your life has ever jacked you off?" And so I

                    57

just did this, I just pushed the cover right back. And I just took hold of his cock, and I started to rub it. And he said to me, he said, "don't put it in your mouth." I said, "oh, well. I really wasn't thinking about it exactly at this moment. But what's your great objection?" He says, "well, I don't know." He says, "just do what you want to do, but don't put it in your mouth."

I mean, don't you love it? But, I mean, it was one of the more interesting sex experiences in my life. He asked me twice did I think he had a really big thing.

                    ANDY
He had a big cock?

                    TRUMAN
It was nice. Nicely proportioned. It was a pretty cock.

                    ANDY
He must have been -- was he -- he must have been adorable.

                    TRUMAN
Oh. He was so sweet. Well, then afterwards, you see, we became the greatest friends in the world. I mean, I think I was probably one of the two or three greatest friends Bogie ever had, in the end of his life, you know. But at this point, this was when I really first knew him.

                        ANDY
Oh, really. Oh.

                        TRUMAN
Oh, I had such weird experiences with these
people.

        (Pause.)

                        TRUMAN
Are you a jealous person, Andy?

                        ANDY
Well, I don't want to be, but I guess I am.

                        TRUMAN
That's my great downfall.

                        ANDY
That's your great downfall?

                        TRUMAN
Yeah. It's funny, I work out with these
therapists, but . . . I mean, it's ridiculous,
it's stupid, it's childish.

                        ANDY
It's stupid.

                        TRUMAN
It's idiotic.

ANDY

I know. Is there a jealous pill? It would be
great. It must be a chemical kind of thing. Or do
you think some people aren't jealous or --

TRUMAN

It's human nature to be jealous. But, of course,
it's related to love. That's all it's got anything
to do with, if you get rid of that, it means you're
not in love with them anymore. That's certainly the
truth with me. You can always tell when the end is
coming, because I'm no longer jealous.

ANDY

Yes. It's true.

TRUMAN

Then you become real good friends. Because
friendship is the perfect sort of trust and belief
and not lying to one another. People who are
having a love-sex relationship are continuously
lying to each other, because you have to make a
love object of this person, which means that you
editorialize about them. You cut out what you
don't want to see, you add what isn't there. And
so therefore you're building a lie.

ANDY

Yeah.

TRUMAN

But in a friendship you don't do that. You do
exactly the reverse. You try more and more to be

as completely pure and straight as you can be. I
mean, you know, like with Jack. But Jack and I
haven't been lovers now for what, 15 years. But
he's still certainly my best friend.

                    ANDY
If Jack is the magic person, why did you leave him?

                    TRUMAN
I never left him.

                    ANDY
Well, but, I mean, why did you need other people
to entertain you?

                    TRUMAN
It isn't a matter of entertaining me or something
like that.

                    ANDY
Oh. It is.

                    TRUMAN
I just got tired of that same old cock. You know,
I just got tired of it.

                    ANDY
Really. How did you ever meet in the first place?
Where did you meet? Here in New York?

                    TRUMAN
He was married to Joan McCracken, who was a friend
of mine.

                    ANDY
Joan McCracken the dancer?

                    TRUMAN
Yes.

                    ANDY
In *Oklahoma!*?

                    TRUMAN
Yes.

                    ANDY
Was he a dancer? He must be a raving beauty. Oh,
God.

                    TRUMAN
Oh. Wait until you see.

                    ANDY
And Joan McCracken? Where is she now?

                    TRUMAN
Dead.

                    ANDY
She died? From what?

                    TRUMAN
She married Bob Fosse and I think that killed her.

                    ANDY
Really? God!

                    62

                    TRUMAN
Anyway, your taste is probably extremely different
from mine.

                    ANDY
My taste?

                    TRUMAN
Your taste I bet is very, very different. I'm sure
the sort of person that you think is attractive
with me is zero.

                    ANDY
Well, I never do anything so -- I mean, no.

                    TRUMAN
What?

                    ANDY
Well, I never do anything so . . .

                    TRUMAN
I don't believe you.

                    ANDY
No, it's true. It's true. I don't do anything.

                    TRUMAN
Well, that's not very healthy.

                    ANDY
I know. It isn't very healthy. That's why I'm
having problems.

TRUMAN

Sex is an awfully strange thing, Andy.

ANDY

I know. Yeah. It is. I'm always -- I'm -- I'm so
scared --

TRUMAN

What?

ANDY

I'm so scared of people now. I mean, oh, no. I
mean, of anybody. I mean, even my -- a person I
know. I just don't -- I mean, you know, people
take -- people take -- You trust people so
easily. You do.

TRUMAN

You've got some problems. I have never been
able quite to put my finger on what it is that's
bothering you. I don't know.

ANDY

Yeah, but the thing is --

TRUMAN

But there's a little kind of curious area there.
And I've decided I don't want to know because you
don't want anybody to know. My life's an open
book. I mean, I do what I do, and I do this and I
do that --

                    ANDY
But I don't do anything. I mean, sex is sort of
funny.

                    TRUMAN
But that's not right, Andy. It's so wrong.

                    ANDY
Well, people kiss and tell. It's so hard.

                    TRUMAN
So. What do you care?

                    ANDY
Well, they do.

                    TRUMAN
You care? I mean, I don't. I couldn't care less.

                    ANDY
Well, kiss and tell, I mean, it's just -- it's
funny.

                    TRUMAN
Well, you're very -- you're very shy, but I don't
know, maybe that's all that is.

                    ANDY
Who did I go to bed with last night, Truman?

                    TRUMAN
Nobody.

                    ANDY
That's right.

                    TRUMAN
That's more than I can say.

                    ANDY
Really.

                    TRUMAN
I must say, I had a fantastic sex life.

                    ANDY
Oh. I used to come home and I'd be so glad to find
a little roach there to talk to. At least somebody
was there to greet you at home, right? And then
they just go away. They're great!

                    TRUMAN
Something must be going wrong in your brain
somewhere!

        (The lights change. ANDY's thoughts:)

                    ANDY
*I think I was twenty-five the first time I had sex.
I stopped at twenty-six. But the first time I ever
knew about sex was in Northside, Pittsburgh, under
the stairs and they made this funny kid suck this
boy off. I never understood what it meant. I was just
sitting there watching. When I was five years old.*

        (The lights restore.)

                    66

                    TRUMAN
Sex can't be everything. I mean, sex is only
15 minutes. And the rest of the time you're
quarreling with somebody and you're -- you know,
what if that's all it is?

                     ANDY
The most exciting thing is not doing it. If you
fall in love with someone and never do it, it's
much more exciting.

                    TRUMAN
Fascinating.

        (The lights change. Video transition. A title
        appears:)

GENERATOR

ANDY
Cab to Truman's apartment at U.N. Plaza. Three
dollars and fifty cents.

(TRUMAN'S apartment. ANDY alone, taking in
the view.)

ANDY
Gee Truman, the layout of this apartment is so
great. It's so beautiful here . . . Oh isn't
sun wonderful? I think sun is the most exciting
thing to have in an apartment. I live in a dark
dump.

(TRUMAN enters. HE is looking at HIS mail
and tossing the sealed envelopes on the floor.
HE is clearly intoxicated.)

ANDY
Truman, you don't even open them?

TRUMAN
Oh. I never open my mail.

ANDY
Oh, really. You mean you just --

                         TRUMAN
I don't ever read it. Do you not believe your own
magazine where it tells you that I don't read my
mail?

                          ANDY
Oh. But I didn't really believe it.

                         TRUMAN
Well, I don't read my mail.

                          ANDY
Can't I save them and put them in our box? I'll
buy them from you. A penny a piece. Can I --

                         TRUMAN
I'll give you all of my mail for free. Would you
like that?

                          ANDY
Could you -- okay. Oh, yeah.

       (ANDY eagerly and carefully picks up each
       piece of mail from the floor.)

                         TRUMAN
You're such a collector.

                          ANDY
Yes, I know. I used to write to you every day,
for years, until your mother told me to stop it?
Remember?

                    TRUMAN
I don't remember my mother doing that, no.

                    ANDY
She did. She called me up and said it. She was
really sweet.

                    TRUMAN
She was drunk. Because my mother really was an
alcoholic.

                    ANDY
But I met your mother.

                    TRUMAN
I know you met my mother. But my mother was a
very ill, awfully eccentric woman, and a total
alcoholic.

                    ANDY
Really? When I met her, she wasn't --

                    TRUMAN
Yes, she was an alcoholic when you met her. She
had been an alcoholic since I was 16, so she was
an alcoholic when you met her.

                    ANDY
I never knew that.

                    TRUMAN
You didn't realize it?

ANDY

No. She was really sweet.

TRUMAN

Well, she had this sort of sweet thing, and then
suddenly she'd . . . well, you know, she committed
suicide.

ANDY

She did? Oh, I didn't know that. I thought she
just got sick.

TRUMAN

No, no, no, no. She committed suicide. She had
this extraordinary sweet quality, but then she
was one of those people who would have two
drinks . . .

ANDY

Some people have the right chemical balances and
some people are missing some chemicals.

TRUMAN

I had the most insecure childhood I know of. My
mother was sixteen years old when she was married.
I was born when she was seventeen. They were
divorced when I was four years old, with a great
deal of bitterness on both sides. We were living
in this hotel in New Orleans. My mother was always
running off to do something or other. She had no
money and no one to leave me with. She would leave
me locked in this hotel room when she went out
in the evening with her beaus and I would become

hysterical because I couldn't get out of this
room. It was really ghastly.

                    ANDY
Life hurts so much.

                    TRUMAN
Something in life has done a terrible hurt to me,
and I think it is irrevocable.

      (Pause.)

I mustn't have anything to drink. I mean -- Well,
we all know all of that. But, on the other hand,
there's a whole other side to that story, too.

                    ANDY
Yes.

                    TRUMAN
I mean, I can go for a month or two months without
drinking. But I just got to drink once in a while.
I drink because it's the only time I can stand it.

                    ANDY
Yeah.

                    TRUMAN
It's better, actually. It's better that I should
drink. But no doctor in the world would ever
believe that. They would say, oh, no. I mean,
you don't drink for two months, et cetera, and
then you drink for two or three days, and then

                    72

they don't understand the sort of nature of
the sensibility, is what it really is. Not the
ailment, the sensibility. I mean, something
has to be turned off. It's like turning off an
extraordinary --

                    ANDY
Yes!

                    TRUMAN
My mind is like a fantastic generator.

                    ANDY
It is. I know. Working every minute. The machinery
is always going. Even when you sleep.

                    TRUMAN
You know, most people's minds are going putt,
putt, putt, putt, putt. My mind is like an
incredible generator. I mean, it's just churning
with incredible impressions, images, stories --
and it has to be turned off once in a while.

                    ANDY
I know. I know. But, see --

                    TRUMAN
It has to be -- it has to be turned off some way or
another.

                    ANDY
I know. But the liquor just turns it on and then
you're --

TRUMAN

It turns it on, but it turns it off. But, I
mean, it's got to be turned off once in a while.
Otherwise, I mean, it's just too --

ANDY

The liquor makes your blood go real fast.

TRUMAN

Nobody can live with this kind of a generator
going in their head all the time.

ANDY

I know. Oh, I know.

TRUMAN

I mean, because it's not -- it's not normal.

ANDY

It's very hard. I know.

TRUMAN

You know, it's like zoom, zoom, zoom, zoom, zoom.
I really do receive about 50 perceptions per
minute. The most people have -- five, at the most.

(The lights change. ANDY's thoughts:)

ANDY

*If someone would really take care of Truman, he
would be okay. I got back some of my pictures of
Truman. He looked like he didn't have any teeth.
Does he have teeth?*

74

(The lights restore.)

                    TRUMAN
The other day, I was lying in bed thinking -- it's
like having a fantastic Ferrari motor running in
your head all the time, and there's speed limits
everywhere, you know. And I can't use this thing.
And it's driving me gradually crazy because the
thing speeds up more and more and more.

                    ANDY
I know. I think you could find a drug that would
stop it a little bit.

                    TRUMAN
Oh. I've tried every --

                    ANDY
No, no. But, I mean -- eventually you will find
that one little thing that would, you know, slow
it down.

                    TRUMAN
Something, just to stop it for a little while. I
mean, I think I have a really great gift, and I
owe it somehow to get it out! I've been writing
professionally for almost forty years. That's a
very long time. A writer can have a long career,
but very few of them actually do. Because it's so
nerve shattering. You're continuously striving and
reaching and being miserable and happy and taking
drugs and drinking and doing something to get out
of this ghastly tension. Because what you're doing

is gambling with your life. It isn't reputation, this is your life, these are the years gone by, and am I wasting them? Have I totally wasted it?

(TRUMAN is in deep pain. ANDY doesn't know what to say. THEY sit in silence for a few moments. Then, with some effort, ANDY reaches out and places HIS hand on TRUMAN'S knee. TRUMAN is calmed and touched by this. TRUMAN pats ANDY'S hand in acknowledgment. ANDY gently pulls away.)

ANDY

Art is too hard.

TRUMAN

I'd just as soon have not been a writer if I'd had a choice. My head is so full of things and ideas. It's a very unusual sort of case I have. You've got a kind of other thing. You're one of the shrewdest people I know --

ANDY

No. I'm not. No. You . . .

TRUMAN

Yes. But we're talking about you.

ANDY

Yeah. I know. No. But --

TRUMAN

We're talking about you.

                    ANDY
I'm not.

                    TRUMAN
No. I want to talk for one minute about you.

                    ANDY
Okay.

                    TRUMAN
Because you're incredibly clever and shrewd.

                    ANDY
No, I'm not. I'm really not.

                    TRUMAN
Yes. You are.

                    ANDY
No, I'm not.

                    TRUMAN
And it's all disguised marvelously.

                    ANDY
If I was, I would be more -- you know, doing more
stuff.

                    TRUMAN
No. But it's everything I am not. I am clever,
shrewd, smart. I have one of the greatest creative
imaginations that's ever been. I got every -- all
the motors running.

                     77

                         ANDY
Yeah. You do.

                       TRUMAN
Everything running in a way that's -- that's not
running with you.

                         ANDY
Mine aren't.

                       TRUMAN
And it's not running.

                         ANDY
It's just --

                       TRUMAN
Your motors are way off.

                         ANDY
Mine are not running.

                       TRUMAN
I mean, they're just barely turning over.

                         ANDY
They're barely turning over.

                       TRUMAN
But with me, I mean --

                         ANDY
They're running.

                          78

                    TRUMAN
The whole thing is running like a total Ferrari
thing going all the time. And you've got something
else. But I don't understand what it is.

                    ANDY
It's true. Mine doesn't run and yours runs. I
don't know either.

          (Pause.)

I'm strange. It's the dents.

                    TRUMAN
Yes. The dents.

          (THEY ponder that for a moment.)

You know, I am -- I consider myself -- with all,
you know, I can say I'm the most intelligent
person that I know --

                    ANDY
Well, you are.

                    TRUMAN
And you're the one person that I don't really
honestly get. I get it all the way up to one point.
Okay. Because I know -- you're extraordinarily
creative. You have a really imaginative --

                    ANDY
Well, that's what it is.

                    79

                    TRUMAN
No, no. Wait. Now let's --

                     ANDY
No, no. But I'm naïve and imaginative. That's
about all.

                    TRUMAN
You know, we're going to get down to number one.

                     ANDY
This is like going to therapy.

                    TRUMAN
We're just going to get down to where the thing
is. You have all of these things and then there's
a sudden drop.

                     ANDY
Well, no.

                    TRUMAN
I mean, it's like a drop -- like a drop in --
in -- well, I don't know. Blood pressure.

                     ANDY
It's true.

                    TRUMAN
So there's this incredible drop that suddenly
stops like you were, let's say --

ANDY

But then let me explain what the -- where the --
oh. I'll explain the magic to you -- I'll tell you
the magic things. I like ideas. It's -- well, I
don't know really. I'm trying to do things. If I
had only stayed with doing the *Campbell's Soup*,
because everybody only does one painting anyway.
Doing it whenever you need money is a really good
idea, just that one painting over and over again,
which is what everybody remembers you for anyway.
I mean, I'm trying. I wake up every morning. I
open my eyes and think: "here we go again." I was
just trying to do newer ideas and stuff like that.
Each idea was just something to do. And, you know,
it's just that we keep trying. It's just all these
nice kids working. I mean, you met them.

TRUMAN

I think all the kids that work with you are
terrific.

ANDY

Oh, yeah. There are like 20 right now. But we had
better ones before.

TRUMAN

I think they're all terrific.

ANDY

But the ones before were really more imaginative.
They didn't make any money at all. Now there's
a difference, you know, since they're really on
salary. It's a different thing. Before I thought

all these crazy kids were imaginative. So anybody
that was peculiar, you know, we would have them
around. Then I was shot. I was shot by Valerie
Solanas at the Factory in '68. . . .

                    TRUMAN
I remember that.

                    ANDY
I mean, it was just . . . It made me feel . . . I
mean, it was really terrible. My lungs are still
funny from being shot.

                    TRUMAN
What a terrible, horrible time.

                    ANDY
It was painful.

                    TRUMAN
Do you remember what happened?

                    ANDY
Oh, yeah. I had just ridden up in the elevator
with her and I turned around to make a telephone
call and just heard noise, that's all. My life
didn't flash in front of me or anything. I just
never think about it.

                    TRUMAN
Insane bitch.

ANDY

After that I stopped seeing creepy people. I don't see imaginative people anymore. It brought back bad memories of getting shot. I got scared.

TRUMAN

Of course.

ANDY

Now, they're not allowed in the door if they're peculiar. So we're not that creative anymore. They're not. I'm not. I don't have strong feelings on anything. I just use whatever happens around me for my material. I just do anything anybody asks me to do. You have to be a business. It all stops being just fun, and then you wonder: what is art? Does it really come out of you, or is it just a product? I should've just done the *Campbell's Soup Cans* and kept on doing them. It's very complicated. You know what I mean.

TRUMAN

Andrew, you are a sterling fellow. And no one ever said differently.

(Pause.)

ANDY

The world fascinates me.

83

                    TRUMAN
I feel that I understand you really. I know so
much better about you than you know about yourself
that you just wouldn't even believe.

        (Pause.)

                    ANDY
Oh, Truman. Thanks a lot. I really have to go walk
the dogs. They -- I've been gone all night and
they're probably tearing up the house, so . . .

                    TRUMAN
Oh, God. Andy, go. Go.

                    ANDY
Okay. Okay. So I'll call you.

                    TRUMAN
I have so much affection and feeling. Andy, you
know how much I love you, right? I care about you
more than you know.

        (ANDY doesn't know how to respond.)

                    ANDY
God. Thanks. Thanks a lot. Gee.

        (The lights change. Video transition. A title
        appears:)

STRANGE DENTS

ANDY

Truman called on Monday and his voice -- I didn't
even know it was him on the phone. He's like one
of those people from outer space -- the body
snatchers -- because it's the same person, but
it's not the same person. He was saying cuckoo
things, like that he'd died twice and that his
brain had stopped for thirty-two seconds, so
that's what he was going to call his next book --
"Thirty-Two Seconds."

(Lights focus on tape recorder. We hear fast-
forward sound. Lights restore to ANDY.)

ANDY

Truman collapsed in his lobby at about 6:30, and
all the newspapers and TV reporters rushed over to
U.N. Plaza. He was taken to the hospital and it
was front-page news. He got the cover of the *Post*
and everything.

(Lights focus on tape recorder. We hear fast-
forward sound. Lights restore to ANDY.)

ANDY

Truman went to a hospital in Miami. You can't stop
people -- if he's going to kill himself, he's
going to do it.

(Lights focus on tape recorder. We hear fast-forward sound. Lights restore to ANDY.)

                    ANDY
Truman died in California.

I didn't go to the funeral.

I got up and played those days with Truman that I'd taped for the play.

I thought I could turn these tapes into plays and they'd be my little fortune, but by talking in them so much myself, I ruined them. I should've just kept my mouth shut.

It's not that I don't like to speak about myself, it's that there really isn't anything to say about me. I'm not saying anything now.

I'm just watching, observing the world.

Truman was a magic person.

        (TRUMAN appears upstage. HE is sober and free of pain. Clear.)

                    TRUMAN
When God does give one a gift, whatever it may be, composing or writing, for whatever pleasure it may bring, it also is a very painful thing to live with. It's a very excruciating life, facing that blank piece of paper every day and having to reach

up somewhere into the clouds and bring something
down out of them.

        (The lights fade on TRUMAN. HE remains
        onstage, gazing at ANDY.)

                ANDY
God.

It's too hard to think about things. I think
people should think less anyway.

Life hurts so much. If we could become more
mechanical, we would be hurt less.

It's too hard to care.

It's so much easier not to care.

Well . . .

I care.

        (The lights fade to black.)

        END OF PLAY

BONUS MATERIAL

CONTENTS

BONUS MATERIAL

WRITING

PLAY

WARHOL: We want to write -- we want to write -- we want to write a new play about three astronauts in space for about 10 days. Wouldn't it be great? What -- what would they do in space?

CAPOTE: But you have -- didn't I ever tell you about my super idea for an erotic movie?

WARHOL: No. What is it?

CAPOTE: Well, these three astronauts get into this thing and they're sent off to the moon, and they travel for days and days and days, and they get hornier and hornier and hornier. And the whole thing turns into one of the all-time sex movies. Where they're inside the capsule on the moon everywhere. They are having a complete ball. And then they finally get back in the capsule and they splash down and -- and

(a former president of the United States)

comes rushing out and says you're so terrific, et cetera. And they go for a swim and they all have a ball there. And that's the end of the movie.

WARHOL: Oh, great.

DIARY

CAPOTE: Well, have you seen

(a famous playwright)'s

diaries?

WARHOL: Oh, yeah.

CAPOTE: You -- we've got them, right?

WARHOL: Do you keep a diary, Truman.

CAPOTE: No.

WARHOL: You don't. You should.

CAPOTE: Yeah. Well, listen, Andy, you see, you know the reason I don't keep a diary?

WARHOL: You have the memory.

CAPOTE: It's -- well, I can, but it's not that. When I want to write something, I want to write it. I mean, I want to write it as a work of art.

WARHOL: Yeah.

CAPOTE: See, keeping a diary is a form of work of art.

WARHOL: Yeah.

CAPOTE: If you are totally concentrating on --

WARHOL: On.

CAPOTE: -- style, and this, and that, and the other. Now, if I kept a diary, then I'd get totally absorbed in this thing. I would spend five hours a day on it. I would be doing it because I have an obsession about how something is done.

WARHOL: It actually -- you know, it actually takes us that long. Because we have to give it to

(an associate of Andy's).

She types it on the typewriter. So it does takes two, three hours a day just to -- You know, it's just not worth it somehow. Just to -- just to -- you know, it's incredible. It takes that long and then she has to type it up and then --

GENIUS

CAPOTE: Well, I make probably -- on a level of -- because it's what I call death by rarity, because I write so little, but when I do, I get more than any other writer in America. I don't care who you're talking --

WARHOL: Yeah.

CAPOTE: I mean, I will be paid more than any writer. Here I am, the one and only real true genius in America.

SEX

BLOWJOB SCHOOL

WARHOL: Oh, Truman, Truman. I got the best idea last night for a school. Remember we were always talking about how to make money and we were doing speed reading? We're doing a school called speed sucking. We have to teach.

CAPOTE: Speed sucking. Yeah, but that's not how it really works.

WARHOL: No, but
                    (wife of a famous rock star)
was telling me how to keep a man that's really, you know, how she keeps
                    (famous rock star)
now is give him a really good blowjob before he goes out on, you know, and then just do it. If you have a minute with your guy, you just give him the best blowjob.

CAPOTE: Uh-huh.

WARHOL: And we thought -- I mean, it would be -- I mean, it would be, you've got to teach people how to really have good -- and remember you don't even know -- kids don't know how to do sex or anything but to have a school on how to do good blowjobs.

CAPOTE: I've written a description of it that says the sensation -- but it's in *Answered Prayers*.

WARHOL: What is it in?

CAPOTE: *Answered Prayers.*

WARHOL: It is?

CAPOTE: There's a description of somebody giving --

WARHOL: Really?

CAPOTE: -- that is exactly like one of the greatest textbooks you've ever seen in your life.

WARHOL: What is that? Oh, really? What does that -- when is that -- oh, really?

CAPOTE: It's the greatest single description of how to keep somebody going and going and going.

WARHOL: Oh, really? Oh, great.

CAPOTE: So you have them completely out of their mind.

WARHOL: Oh, great.

RELATIONSHIPS

CAPOTE: He is the world's greatest computer expert.

WARHOL: Really? I didn't know that.

CAPOTE: He does all the computers for Westinghouse and IBM and anything hard, because he's the greatest. I mean, he's fantastic.

WARHOL: Really. Does he suck cock?

CAPOTE: That's why he's so incredibly ill --

WARHOL: Does -- does

(a boyfriend of Truman's)

suck cock?

CAPOTE: What?

WARHOL: Does

(a boyfriend of Truman's)

suck cock?

CAPOTE: With me, he'll do anything.

WARHOL: Really? How sweet. God.

CAPOTE: With me, he'll do any -- I'll tell you the truth, you know.

WARHOL: Yeah, but I mean -- well, then he probably never did -- never would have done anything with anybody else.

CAPOTE: Well, it's not exactly what you would call his deal.

WARHOL: No. But he -- he probably never had an affair with anybody else. Did he?

CAPOTE: No. He's --

WARHOL: You're probably -- no, you're probably the only person --

CAPOTE: No. I -- at least I don't know. So far as I knew -- I don't know nothing. He's been married twice. He has six children.

WARHOL: Yeah, but he never probably had an affair with anybody. You're probably his first, I'm sure.

CAPOTE: I don't know.

WARHOL: No, he looked so good today.

CAPOTE: But he's very honest.

WARHOL: I know. He got -- looked so good today. I mean, I've never seen him look so good. He's adorable.

CAPOTE: He's very honest. He's a very honest, very -- very straight person, you know.

WARHOL: He's really adorable. Does he get hurt that you don't go home with him? I mean, because --

CAPOTE: No. He was glad I didn't go.

WARHOL: Why? You mean you can be asleep and then you can just --

CAPOTE: No. I go to bed, I go to sleep. When I come, I go to bed and --

WARHOL: He watches TV?

CAPOTE: No, no. He doesn't do anything.

WARHOL: Really. Oh.

CAPOTE: He just -- he works so hard.

WARHOL: Oh, really.

CAPOTE: I mean, honestly, truly he really gets up at 5:00 o'clock in the -- well, even, I mean, 4:30, 5:00 o'clock, whatever.

WARHOL: Really.

CAPOTE: And he works all the way through.

WARHOL: Does he wake you up in the morning?

CAPOTE: No. He always says --

WARHOL: When does he get to go to his uptown apartment?

CAPOTE: And then he always says, you know --

WARHOL: When does he go up to his uptown apartment?

CAPOTE: Oh, he has an apartment. He has a very pretty apartment.

WARHOL: When does he go up there?

CAPOTE: What? Oh. Well, he goes up there to get something or other and then he comes down.

WARHOL: Oh.

CAPOTE: And then he gets back in bed with me and -- I mean, he's adorable.

WARHOL: Oh, he is adorable.

CAPOTE: He's the most adorable. I mean, he's adorable.

WARHOL: I think he's great. Yeah, he's great.

CAPOTE: Because, you know, he gets in bed with me and later on he says, are you about to be awake or a little bit awake or whatever? I say, oh, I don't want to be awake.

WARHOL: How old is

(a boyfriend of Truman's)?

CAPOTE: He's 46.

WARHOL: Oh, really. Oh. He's so handsome for a -- he looks much younger. No, he does.

CAPOTE: He's 46.

WARHOL: Yeah, he really looks great.

CAPOTE: He's 46. He has the -- he has -- he has six of the most beautiful children you ever saw in your life.

WARHOL: Oh, really. Oh. They're all redheads or --

CAPOTE: No.

WARHOL: Yeah. He's really a redhead.

CAPOTE: He's married to a real dumb --

WARHOL: Did you ever fight with her?

CAPOTE: What?

WARHOL: Did you ever have a fight? Did she ever have -- no -- she doesn't --

CAPOTE: I have only had -- I've had -- in my life -- I've only had three lovers, I mean, serious lovers. All of whom were married. And -- but I never had no quarrels with their wives at all. At all.

WARHOL: But what do you think of -- do you think -- why -- why else --

CAPOTE: Nothing. I mean, they -- they left and they came and that was it.

WARHOL: But do you think -- do you think he was unhappy for 20 years being married? I mean, he must have been. He must have been --

CAPOTE: Well, he was married twice.

WARHOL: Was he tortured? I mean, do you think he was a tortured person?

CAPOTE: He was married -- no -- he was married twice.

WARHOL: And he liked -- he was happy being married and everything like that?

CAPOTE: Oh, no. You see, he's absolutely straight, as they call it, in that terrible boring way.

WARHOL: What do you -- why -- how can you say that?

CAPOTE: Well, he just is.

WARHOL: How?

CAPOTE: Then I met -- see, I can do things to people.

WARHOL: But I mean --

CAPOTE: Well, I have done it three times.

WARHOL: Yeah. But I mean --

CAPOTE: So I certainly can do it.

WARHOL: Yeah. But you told me -- you told me that you found

(a boyfriend of Truman's)

at a cocktail, you know, where --

CAPOTE: I met him at a party -- place.

WARHOL: With other men and stuff like that. And you knew that he was carrying on with other men.

CAPTOE: Every single person that I ever did, that's in --

WARHOL: Yeah. But I mean --

CAPOTE: Every single one of them. I never met them under any other circumstances.

WARHOL: No, no. But I mean -- no, but I mean, I mean, I know a lot of married men that, you know, could go to the -- you know, the wives and stuff like that, and carry on and they go home and stuff like --

CAPOTE: But that's not -- I'm not interested in that. And any -- and then -- first of all --

WARHOL: No. But I mean -- but he must have been that kind of person. I mean, if he --

CAPOTE: He never even heard about it.

WARHOL: No. But he -- if -- if he turned then, I mean, he must have thought about it. I mean --

CAPOTE: He never even heard of it. He didn't even know that anything existed.

WARHOL: Why?

CAPOTE: He never even knew that -- that there was such a thing that even existed.

WARHOL: Is he -- is he then thinking that he's a doctor and is helping you or priest? Or what is he thinking he's doing?

CAPOTE: Are we talking about

(a boyfriend of Truman's)?

WARHOL: Yeah.

CAPOTE: Here tonight?

WARHOL: Yeah. What does he think he's doing then?

CAPOTE: No. We're just having a fantastic sex affair.

WARHOL: But I mean --

CAPOTE: No. Nothing. I just --

WARHOL: You expect him --

CAPOTE: I just think he's terrifically attractive.

WARHOL: Yeah, he's terrific. But do you think he's going to -- you expect him to leave soon or --

CAPOTE: He'll never leave.

WARHOL: See, I know. Well --

CAPOTE: He'll never leave. He would no sooner leave me than -- I think -- I don't -- There are a couple of people -- see, I have a lot of people in my life.

WARHOL: But -- but -- but then -- how could he be -- you said he is straight. How could he be straight if he's doing what he's doing?

CAPOTE: He would never leave me.

WARHOL: But if he's doing this, he can't be --

CAPOTE: The only person that I ever had an affair with that left for somebody else -- but then they came back. Oh, boy, did they come back.

WARHOL: Who was that?

CAPOTE: But it's the only time in my whole life that something -- somebody did. And that was

(another, earlier boyfriend of Truman's).

WARHOL: Oh.

CAPOTE: He -- he -- there was a friend of mine with -- I don't know. I don't know, I mean, he's crazy, anyway. He's totally mad. And I had this friend who was an extremely rich girl, also, extremely intelligent. And she -- for some reason --

WARHOL: So he left -- he left you for another girl?

CAPOTE: He left me for her.

WARHOL: And who was that?

CAPOTE: Her name was

(a non-celebrity female).

And he -- but he regretted that. Ha, ha, ha, did he ever regret that. You know, I mean, and I -- but she was an attractive girl. She was very rich. But, now, you see,

(another, earlier boyfriend of Truman's)

was fabulous in bed. I mean really fabulous. More than anybody I've ever known in my life. More --

WARHOL: What did he do that was so fabulous? I don't understand.

CAPOTE: Oh, he was really fantastic.

WARHOL: What did he do?

CAPOTE: I mean really fantastic.

WARHOL: He had a big cock. Okay. That was great.

CAPOTE: Oh, well. That goes without --

WARHOL: But what -- okay. But what did he do that was so fabulous? I don't want to --

CAPOTE: He just was fantastic. He just really did the whole -- he did a really great job --

WARHOL: Of what?

CAPOTE: Top to bottom. And he was incredible. I -- I think (another, earlier boyfriend of Truman's) was the single best person I've ever been -- went to bed with in my life.

WARHOL: Really?

CAPOTE: And I'll give him top mark.

WARHOL: Well, what is a good fuck?

CAPOTE: And the second person I'll give is --

WARHOL: Was (a longtime prior boyfriend of Truman's)

CAPOTE: No, no,

(another, earlier boyfriend of Truman's)

is something special because he's sort of -- he's great.

WARHOL: Truman, what -- what is -- Truman, what is -- tell me -- tell me --

CAPOTE: But the second person is -- which is our friend tonight --

WARHOL: But somebody -- what is a good fuck? You have to tell me. What is one? What is -- what is it?

CAPOTE: Well, our friend tonight --

WARHOL: Yeah, but what is it?

CAPOTE: I tell you it's absolutely out of this world.

WARHOL: What is -- what -- what makes it out of this world? Is it --

CAPOTE: Well --

WARHOL: It takes two hours? A minute? A week? Five minutes?

CAPOTE: Oh, no. I mean, he's just a fantastic -- you know, he's just fantastic. He's really great. He just -- he starts with your eyebrows, and he just does this thing slowly, all the way down, all the way -- He has an absolutely fantastically beautiful cock. I mean, really beautiful. If you care about that sort of thing. But I do.

WARHOL: So what -- what --

CAPOTE: He's got one of the most beautiful cocks you've ever seen in the world. Sort of like -- it's like, you know, about 11, 11 and a half inches long. And it's one of those Irish things, and it's long and it's all -- it's terrific. And it's as thick as your wrist.

WARHOL: And it's not prema --

CAPOTE: What?

WARHOL: Premature ejaculations.

CAPOTE: Oh, good God. No. It takes you almost a half an hour to bring him off.

WARHOL: A half an hour? Why a half an hour?

CAPOTE: I don't know why. You see, one thing is that I won't let anybody fuck me.

WARHOL: You don't?

CAPOTE: Because I just -- I just can't stand -- it bores me to death.

WARHOL: What -- what do you do in a half an hour?

CAPOTE: Oh. I did -- I just blow him. You want -- I mean, you want to know the whole damn thing, already?

WARHOL: Yes. But I mean --

CAPOTE: Okay. So, I mean, he's got a beautiful body. He maybe doesn't look like it does -- that he does when you're looking, but he really actually does. He has an absolutely really beautiful body. He has one of the most beautiful pricks you're ever going to see in your life. I mean, really -- Well, I don't know. See, the one thing I really like to do is, I just like to -- I just like to neck or kiss or doing things for a long, long time. Then I'll do the thing -- by that time, I got the person so worked up that it really doesn't really take very much time.

WARHOL: Don't you fall asleep?

CAPOTE: Oh, all -- I mean, almost immediately.

WARHOL: You do.

CAPOTE: Almost immediately. And, you know -- I don't know -- I got this thing, you know, I don't -- all the people -- all -- that I've ever had this real -- I don't have casual sex affairs with people. I don't have -- I really truly don't. Not at all. It doesn't interest me in the least. I think -- for instance, about him --

WARHOL: I bet you're the first person who he's gone to bed with.

CAPOTE: Well, it's -- no. It's not that -- but it's --

WARHOL: He's had other people? Boys?

CAPOTE: But he came to see me, on one night, five times.

WARHOL: He came five times?

CAPOTE: No, no. Five times before I finally --

WARHOL: Oh, really?

CAPOTE: -- said -- well, however, I made my little move -- movement about it. I know exactly how I made my little movement about it, but -- and it was fascinating. Because -- because I knew all the time that he was -- when is he going to do this thing. I mean, when is he going to make some -- and I didn't know myself truly. Because I was sort of -- well, maybe, maybe not. Maybe this, maybe this, maybe that. I'm not going to get -- bother with somebody --

WARHOL: Did you ever get

(a famous photographer)?

CAPOTE: Oh.

WARHOL: No, but why -- why -- okay. Why was the illusion broken about

(a famous photographer)?

I mean, he was somebody interesting. The right type, the right look. When -- when did you really -- I mean, no -- I -- I could say the same thing about him, because I -- you know, you -- after a while, you just sort of turn off, right. Something about him -- I don't know -- everything --

CAPOTE: Oh, but he's so boring.

WARHOL: But not at the beginning. When you first meet him, he's -- he's interesting.

CAPOTE: Oh, no.

WARHOL: No?

CAPOTE: He was boring to me right from the word go.

WARHOL: Right the first minute? Oh, really? Oh. But I thought you told me you took -- you took him to the baths and everything like that.

CAPOTE: I did.

WARHOL: And he made out in the baths and everything?

CAPOTE: Umm-hmm. He did.

WARHOL: He did?

CAPOTE: In New Orleans.

WARHOL: Really?

CAPOTE: But to me, terrifically boring. I mean, I think he's so unsexy.

WARHOL: Why is that? I don't know -- I'm --

CAPOTE: Because he's just not -- see, I think a person like --

WARHOL: I don't know. I mean, he looks --

CAPOTE: I think

(a boyfriend of Truman's)

is sexy.

WARHOL: Oh, yeah, real sexy.

DOCKS AND BARS

WARHOL: Oh, Truman, you -- we have to take you to the docks. It's the -- we've had the best time in New York. You have to --

110

CAPOTE: What?

WARHOL: To the docks. Have you been to the docks in New York? All those new places to go to. It's not -- you would love it.

CAPOTE: Well, I haven't been in New York, except on and off for just a few days for the last six months.

WARHOL: You'll have to get a whole -- I'll get you a whole outfit of leather. And it's so great. You can just go -- it -- you couldn't believe it. It's so much fun. There's places called, like, The Strap, The Toilet. I mean, it's --

CAPOTE: Oh. I've read all about that, Andy.

WARHOL: No, but when you see it. I mean, it's unbelievable. They're bars. There's like 15, 20 bars. They're on the dock.

CAPOTE: Oh, wait. They're all the way down at the water.

WARHOL: And it's -- it's so -- I mean, the bars are the most beautiful things in the world. You know, you could have the best drinks, and nobody bothers you. But it's so peculiar. It's just -- the whole thing is peculiar. You get -- you get -- you get show business and everything. I mean, it's just -- I mean, it's just so unbelievable. It just all opened. Yeah. For the last, you know, year or so.

CAPOTE: Well, gosh --

WARHOL: But it gets bigger and bigger. An S&M discotheque.

CAPOTE: I've been going to them for the last 15 years. What's the famous one called, The Eagle? The Eagle's Nest.

WARHOL: Yeah. Well, that was -- well, that was the first one. Yeah. But now there's like 15, 20 and they go, you know -- I mean, they just keep going. I mean, it's just so incredible.

CAPOTE: They have a wrinkle bar in New York. It's famous.

WARHOL: What's a wrinkle bar?

CAPOTE: Oh, Andy. I thought you were really with it. A wrinkle bar is where people go who want to meet really old, old men. They've got some sort of fixation, I mean, you know, high society.

WARHOL: What's the -- what's the -- What's a wrinkle -- what is a wrinkle -- what's a wrinkle

CAPOTE: It's -- it's -- there's one in New York. It's called -- it's -- it's the actual name of the bar. It's in New York.

WARHOL: It's called wrinkle?

CAPOTE: It's called The Waxworks. And it's -- there are people -- there's a whole cult of people who like only really, really old men. I mean, this is both boys and girls. I mean, they like really old men. I mean, you know, 70 -- 70 and up. And so they go there and these very attractive people come there and they just pick up these incredibly, extraordinary old -- I went there once with somebody. Just because I didn't believe them is why I went. I thought they weren't -- that they were making it up. And I went.

WARHOL: Well, all these places -- these places in New York are just unbelievable. I mean, that's why you go, because it's unbelievable.

CAPOTE: But you know the -- the city in this country that's got just everything going on. You know, for every other block, I mean --

WARHOL: What city?

CAPOTE: It's San Francisco.

WARHOL: Really? Oh.

CAPOTE: I mean, San Francisco literally every other block there's some bar that has some specialty. I've been to a bar there called The Corral. And you would -- you walk into the place and you would not believe what is going on in this room. Right in -- in front of the bar. Right in this lighted --

WARHOL: Oh. Have you been there?

CAPOTE: But the whole point about this -- or this particular bar is that everybody in it is an -- a voyeur or exhibitionist. And so they got all into some very deep thing together. Because they're all doing these extraordinary things for the benefit of the voyeurs.

WARHOL: But, Truman, The Toilet is -- Well, The Toilet is the best. They want -- they want anybody to come in. Truman. Truman. The Toilet is great. Because they want anybody to come, they want everybody to come. And they have these -- they have rubber mats on the floor. It's just so unbelievable. You just can't believe -- I mean, it's just -- it's just so unbelievable. You can't believe it. And it's up --

CAPOTE: Well, if you can't believe it, then I'm sure that I'll find the visit --

WARHOL: No. You know who took me is -- is

(an heiress and actress),

who is so interested in all that. And she --

CAPOTE: Who?

WARHOL: And she -- she dresses up, she puts her hair under a leather hat. And she just took -- just took us down. It was so interesting. Gee. And it's -- and -- and it's not on the first floor. You take an elevator.

CAPOTE: Well, I --

WARHOL: They want everybody to really go. It's -- they want to make all the money, really in a rush somehow.

CAPOTE: Well, they open and close so fast. They're open for five months and then wham, something happens.

WARHOL: They raid them.

CAPOTE: The only time that I ever go downtown, because I never go downtown for any of those bars. Because, actually, as a matter of fact, they really bore me. And they bore me for two reasons. One is, even if I found it interesting, nobody leaves me alone for one minute.

WARHOL: Oh, I know. That's, you know --

CAPOTE: I mean, they just close in on you like this. And then they come in and say, "oh, I want an autograph for my little sister."

WARHOL: You know, if -- if you go to those regular bars, they'll come up to you and say woof-woof.

CAPOTE: Well, that wasn't precisely what -- you know.

WARHOL: Oh, I know. It's just so --

CAPOTE: It's awful. And this one -- the most amusing thing -- there was this famous one about five years ago in New York. And you went up in sort of like a feed elevator. And it had five huge rooms. And it was really a wild, wild place.

And

(a friend of Truman's)

-- do you know him?

WARHOL: Yeah.

CAPOTE: Said, "You've got to see this place. If you don't, you know -- because I really do not go anywhere like this for all those reasons." So I said, "all right." So, we had dinner. So, we went up in the elevator -- in the elevator there were about 20 people. All of whom turned around doing that, oh, it's Truman Capote's routine. And that already ruined everything.

WARHOL: Yeah.

SEX CLUB

WARHOL: But, Truman, I have to tell you about this club I went to. After I left Studio 54, it was like 2:30, we walked down the street and it said "guys, dolls." So, we went in. And I don't know if I told you that. And as we went in, one of the waitresses said, "Oh, my God." You know, and so she gave us a seat. It was like -- it was all red. It was like that room in there, it was all red. With a long table, it looked like a roulette table. And there were a few men sitting around at the table. And then there were girls on this table in funny positions. Their asshole was like an inch away from the guy's nose, and their cunt was an inch away from the other guy's nose. I mean, they were in positions -- I mean, and shaking it like --

CAPOTE: Oh, but that's --

WARHOL: It was -- I mean, I was --

CAPOTE: But that's -- that was in doing a bar number.

WARHOL: Yeah. Well, it's not like a bar. It's just a table.

CAPOTE: Yeah, but I know what you're talking about.

WARHOL: It's just incredible. I never saw it in my whole -- I mean, the girls would be -- you know -- and then the girls all came over and they wanted drinks. So, the drinks were 8.50, I didn't know it. So we bought -- all the girls came over. We had like 10 girls. One of them was interested in

(an heiress and actress).

And they said, "Upstairs, you know, you could have a better time." And -- but it was just too weird. And we all -- we left -- we went to a movie next door and saw a glory hole movie, which was so strange and interesting and -- it's just right down the street from Studio 54. I mean, we had the best time. But the girls on the table, it was so weird. I mean, it was actually weird.

MORE THAN I GET

WARHOL: Do you want a drink?

CAPOTE: I don't know. You want to go in there or no?

WARHOL: Oh, I don't know. No, no. It's late.

        (a boyfriend of Truman's)

is probably waiting for you.

CAPOTE: Huh?

WARHOL: You can get that big 12-inch cock. That's more than I get.

WORK

CLUB

CAPOTE: Well, I'm thinking that's a whole other story.
No. It's not hard work if we get
(manager of well-known nightclub).
I mean, I'm not about to run this place, or neither are
you, Andy.

WARHOL: But --

CAPOTE: He has run
(a very well-known nightclub)
for 18 years with great success. I mean --

WARHOL: It's the longest discotheque in New York. It's
the longest -- longest running one.

CAPOTE: And
(manager of well-known nightclub)
has been running it for 18 years. Now, he knows this
whole thing backward, forward. He knows everything.

WARHOL: What should the decoration be? I mean, you
have to think of --

CAPOTE: What?

WARHOL: What should the decorations be?

CAPOTE: Well, that's a whole other thing we can think
about. But that's not the point. I mean, I'm really
talking about practical things.

WARHOL: Just simple? Just a room.

CAPOTE: You open it in and we -- like in April -- and we
push it, and we push it, and we push it, and we get everybody there. And we will make a fortune.

WARHOL: Cash.

CAPOTE: We can sit upstairs counting the cash out every
night. You know, there are very few ways to make an
extraordinary amount of money easily and that's one
of them.

WARHOL: Do you know any --

CAPOTE: I mean, for Christ's sake, if we don't have the
cache to make a place a big success, I don't know who
does.

WARHOL: Do you know anybody in the Mafia? Did you
ever have any Mafia friends?

CAPOTE: Do you think -- do you think Studio 54 would
have been a success if we hadn't all been pushing it? It
wouldn't. It wouldn't.

WARHOL:

>(a publicist)

is still there. She calls people up. She's very good.

CAPOTE: We were all -- we were all pushing it.

>(a rock star's wife),

me,

>(a famous fashion designer).

WARHOL: I wonder how did it all happen? Did we like it there first?

CAPOTE: The point is that if we get our own people together, we open this place. We're going to make a fortune. I'd like to make a fortune. Why not?

TOUR

CAPOTE: -- I mean, you see just having done this tour of this university. Now, that's something that once in a while you ought to do. And there's only one reason to do it. Not about making the money, not about -- you can make an awful lot of money.

WARHOL: Just seeing what the kids -- the kids there want.

CAPOTE: No, it's not. It's really a tremendous amount of hard work. Or at least it is for me. Maybe it wouldn't be so much for you, but -- you see come -- you see a certain real reality about what these people are really thinking. And see, you know, we live in a kind of a somewhat dream world, you know, and we don't --

WARHOL: Well, do the kids have --

CAPOTE: Or we don't really get anything, but doing a tour like that, you know, you really get to see what these people actually truly think. And what they act -- really admire and what is going on in their heads and everything. Now, this is a terribly small part. I mean, I could give you 100 things I learned from that trip about -- but *Rolling Stone* is out.

WARHOL: It is?

CAPOTE: They couldn't care less about *Rolling Stone*. Well, the last tour I ever did, which was about three, four years ago, I mean, *Rolling Stone* was --

WARHOL: Well, what do they read now?

CAPOTE: They love *High Times*. I mean, it's very amusing.

WARHOL: Yeah.

CAPOTE: You see they all know that *Rolling Stone* is out. *Rolling Stone* is a -- a zero. And I think the moment that *Rolling Stone* moved from San Francisco to New York, that was the end of *Rolling Stone*. I really think so. For some reason -- and I haven't quite -- they all love *High Times* and I've decided that they like it because of the title, the name of it. But it's -- it's definitely on everybody's coffee table.

WARHOL: But I like the way you said -- -when I said *High Times*, you said yes. Without even --

CAPOTE: What?

WARHOL: When I asked you for the *High Times*, you said yes without even thinking about it. I mean, you know, I -- but, I mean, *High Times* is -- it's a funny magazine. Do you read it at all? It's very --

CAPOTE: Oh, I've seen it a lot, quite a lot.

WARHOL: It's very strange.

CAPOTE: Strange.

WARHOL: Yeah, it's -- it really is.

CAPOTE: But it's amusing. I like it.

WARHOL: But they never sell very well. They don't sell a lot. They claim 750,000. But then I think Tony said they only actually sell like 200. Well, I don't know. Something like that.

CAPOTE: Well, anyway, the college kids all like it. They all think it's terrific.

WARHOL: They must like it. It must do really well. What do the kids ask also?

CAPOTE: I don't do -- I don't do that.

WARHOL: You don't do -- you don't? What do you do? Just read from -- you give them a talk?

CAPOTE: You want a --

WARHOL: Yes.

CAPOTE: In a two-minute appraisee of what I do.

WARHOL: How about a 30 minute?

CAPOTE: No. A two minute. I mean, even a 60 second.

WARHOL: Okay.

CAPOTE: Okay. First of all, we have the auditorium perfectly set up with a -- I have a lectern with exactly the right kind of light on it or not and --

WARHOL: Do you have to rehearse for that? Do you come in early?

CAPOTE: I have somebody that goes in and they know exactly what it is that I want.

WARHOL: Oh, really. You have a stand, that's great.

CAPOTE: So the lights go dim, the president of the university walks on there and all he says is -- because this is all I want them to say -- "Ladies and gentlemen, this evening we have with us Mr. Truman Capote." He walks off the stage. All the lights in the entire auditorium dim. Usually we have about somewhere between 5 and 8,000 people, all the mikes and whatnot. And I walk on, and I walk on very fast. I mean, so fast you just -- I'm there before you even know I'm there.

WARHOL: Yeah.

CAPOTE: And then I'm there. And I make a little sort of thank you for coming speech, but real brief. And then I go and I read three pieces. I vary the -- but I comment on them before and after. What I do -- and the last one -- I either finish with a story of mine called "A Christmas Memory" or "The Thanksgiving Visitor," because if I've lost them somewhere along the line, I'll get them there.

WARHOL: Yeah.

CAPOTE: You know, if I've lost them, I'll really get them. And I finish that, and as the thing finishes -- the thing and the lights go completely black, I walk off the stage and they do their number. They either stand up or they don't stand up. Sometimes they do; sometimes they don't.

WARHOL: Really, you mean sometimes they clap and some --

CAPOTE: Oh, no, no, no, no. I mean, I get a big [clapping sound]. But, I mean, sometimes they all come up.

WARHOL: Oh, oh, oh.

CAPOTE: You know, and sometimes they don't. You never know. It really doesn't have anything to do with how good you were or whatever, it follows the temperament of whatever the landscape is.

WARHOL: And how long does this take?

CAPOTE: Two hours. And then I come back. I stand in the wings of the thing and all the lights and everything in the place -- and I stand there and I count to 30. And then I come back real fast and I just -- and I do a thing like this. Don't bang -- I just do a thing like this, you know.

And then I walk to the microphone and I say, "Thank you so much for coming this evening. I've enjoyed doing this for you. Goodnight." And I walk off real fast. And that's it.

WARHOL: And then where do you go? Right back to your hotel room?

CAPOTE: Right.

WARHOL: You don't have to go to a party?

CAPOTE: Well, they always have one, but I don't go to them because it's just too exhausting.

WARHOL: Exhausting, yeah. And then do the kids --

CAPOTE: It's a real hard thing to do two hours all by yourself on a stage.

WARHOL: Do kids -- do kids -- do some kids come to the hotel? Do you have to fight them off?

CAPOTE: No, no, no. We turn off everything.

WARHOL: Oh, really. Oh, good.

CAPOTE: It's -- it's not easy. I'll tell you that. It's not easy.

WARHOL: No. What are the three --

CAPOTE: The performance in itself isn't hard.

WARHOL: What are the other two pieces that you do?

CAPOTE: They aren't -- they aren't hard, but it's all the things before --

WARHOL: Before, yeah.

CAPOTE: You know, that -- it's hard. It's too much.

WARHOL: Just getting there.

CAPOTE: In one week, I was doing one after the other, one night after the other. Montana, Wyoming, Boulder, Seattle, Colorado, Oregon. They pay you a lot to do it, but that's really not the point. I do think one should do it once in a while for the reasons that I just told you. Because you get so insulated and isolated, you know, and you really don't know what's going on. And when I do these things, I do find out what people -- is going on in their heads and what they think about this, that and the other. And it's good. At least, I find something odd about it. But, you know, leading this certain kind of -- you really don't know too much. You get so -- and you get really bad, screwy ideas about yourself.

PEOPLE

(A MEMBER OF THE MANSON FAMILY)

WARHOL: Your article is fascinating with

(a member of the Manson Family).

CAPOTE: Isn't that good?

WARHOL: Yeah.

CAPOTE: See, that's the kind of thing I want to do each issue.

WARHOL: Yeah. Yeah.

CAPOTE: I mean, the -- each one will have a -- be -- it will be like a small play.

WARHOL: Oh, yeah. Oh, yeah.

CAPOTE: In which you see everything about a person.

WARHOL: It's great. Oh, yeah. It's a great play.

CAPOTE: Which is -- that's -- that's real art that went into that. That's not meandering, you know.

WARHOL: Yeah. Yeah. I know. I know. It's really great.

CAPOTE: Isn't it good?

WARHOL: Yeah. It's really good.

CAPOTE: Because, you know -- and also the extraordinary thing about that thing is --

WARHOL: I'm surprised that you know all of those people. How do you know all those people?

CAPOTE: Well, I know such a -- because I studied the case and interviewed them all.

WARHOL: Really? Oh.

CAPOTE: Yeah. But -- but, you know, one of the fascinating things to me is that for the very first time, in that interview, is the revelation of what the Manson murders were really all about.

WARHOL: Oh. I know. Yeah.

CAPOTE: You see, it's never been printed before.

WARHOL: Yeah.

CAPOTE: It's always been this nonsense about this righteous war and whatnot.

WARHOL: But do you know -- isn't it funny? I mean --

CAPOTE: And it was all just because -- all because Charlie Manson had a great crush on

(a member of the Manson Family).

WARHOL: Yeah. But isn't it funny to be sent for life -- isn't he in for life for one person of it?

CAPOTE: Yes. But he'll get it -- but he will get a -- he will be paroled. Well, I mean, paroled eventually.

WARHOL: Oh, really.

CAPOTE: Not that he should be, because he's a real menace.

WARHOL: Oh, really? Do you think so? Oh.

CAPOTE: Well, if you really read it. Well, you read it, what he says there at the end.

WARHOL: Yeah. Oh, yeah. I know. Yeah.

CAPOTE: Don't you really like that ending? And --

WARHOL: Yeah. Yeah. Oh, yeah.

CAPOTE: "And it was all good. It was all good."

WARHOL: Oh, yeah.

CAPOTE: I mean, that's really a great ending. He said it like a diminuendo on a piece of music.

(A VERY FAMOUS ROCK STAR)

CAPOTE: I saw

(a very famous rock star)

in Las Vegas.

WARHOL: Did you just recently, or just this last time?

CAPOTE: Last year. He once gave a dinner party for me.

WARHOL: Really.

CAPOTE: And do you want to hear who was at this dinner party?

WARHOL: Yeah.

CAPOTE: Because it was absolutely fascinating. I couldn't imagine who he was going to have between the shows. I'm talking about last year in Las Vegas.

(a very famous rock star),

who I've known a long time, asked me to come down to his opening. And he said, "I just want you to know I'm having a dinner party for you." Because he never gives a dinner party or nothing, I couldn't imagine what it was going to be. So -- wait until you hear. So we go downstairs, and they had a little dining room set up off of his dressing room. It was all very nice, kind of down home. There were six boys in this room, all of whom are part of his entourage, and one woman. And you would never -- if you thought a million years, you would never guess who this woman was. I'll tell you.

(one of the richest women in the world)!

WARHOL: Oh. That's great.

CAPOTE: How about that for a real weird surprise?

WARHOL: That's great.

CAPOTE: And she had flown all the way from Hawaii.

WARHOL: Gee. And she's nice, isn't she? I met her through

(female member of famous American family).

(female member of famous American family)

had her over one day.

CAPOTE:

(one of the richest women in the world)
is all right. That was the entire dinner party. But isn't
it weird?

WARHOL: Yeah.

CAPOTE:

(a very famous rock star)
is smart. He's clever. He's a very amusing conversation.

WARHOL: I never understand --

CAPOTE: I don't understand how he can stand to have all
of these dummies --

WARHOL: No. But everybody always says he likes boys
and stuff. And then --

CAPOTE: What?

WARHOL: Everybody always says he likes boys. And then,
it's not true. I don't know.

CAPOTE: I don't know. It's all he ever has around him. In
Palm Springs, I've seen him many times at his house.
He always has slews of, sort of, hillbilly, rangy types.

WARHOL: Oh. Is he intelligent? I mean, is he really cute?

CAPOTE: Oh.

WARHOL: Is he cute or --

CAPOTE: Well, I like

(a very famous rock star).

He is very amusing. He has terrible, corny friends. But, you know,

(a very famous rock star)

is one of those sort of entourage people. You know, and I don't think he can exist separately or the person --

WARHOL: I read yesterday -- I guess the wife is leaving him or something.

CAPOTE: Oh, well. She was never anything to begin with. I mean, she might as well have been working as a scullery maid downstairs for all of the medics. Out in P. Springs, I mean, he comes over to see me quite often. He comes to me alone. But then he just sits by the pool.

(a very famous rock star)

has talked to me about

(famous manager of a very famous rock star)

at great length. And

(wife of famous manager of a very famous rock star).

He can't stand either one of them. He doesn't -- can't stand him. I know them both very well. But he's -- but he's a kind of a captive. Because he's smart enough to know -- Listen, he would have been out of business 15 years ago if it hadn't been for

(famous manager of a very famous rock star).

And he knows that. He's no dope. But he hasn't any very interesting -- I don't -- the only thing I can ever talk to him about is he tells me funny stories about -- of these films he's made and the scripts. And he's very cynical. He's very, very cynical.

WARHOL: But when was

(famous manager of a very famous rock star)

going to put him in something a little better? I mean, you know, I mean, up until now, it's that certain kind of movie he does over and over again.

CAPOTE: Oh. Well, their theory -- that whole theory now is that

(a very famous rock star)

will only tour for now. And then make records. And he's not going -- he's not going to make any films.

WARHOL: Oh. They're not -- I mean, they won't try to make him better or, you know, like a --

CAPOTE: Well, you see, the point was that he always had a -- a flat fee. He never took any part of participation. He had an absolutely flat fee. And the fee was $1,000,000. That was it.

WARHOL: Yeah. But he can get a movie -- he probably can get a movie . . .

CAPOTE: Nobody can get $1,000,000 up-front anymore. Nobody can. You know, in Palm Springs there's -- there's -- he comes to Palm Springs. He has maybe, I would say, four or five times over the past four years he's rung me up and said would I like to have dinner with him. And he knows that I won't come to that house. Or with those people, because they just bore -- and they're oh, so boring. I mean, really unbelievable. But there is this terrible restaurant in a place called Cathedral City, which is -- you know where that is.

WARHOL: Yeah.

CAPOTE: It's called the Rainbow Room, and it's a Chinese restaurant, and it's just ghastly. And I've been there four times to dinner with him, because it's the only place that he will go. I mean, he -- he's one of those people of total habit. He will only -- he claims he doesn't drink, you know, but he does.

WARHOL: Oh, he doesn't drink?

CAPOTE: Oh. He does drink. He -- but -- but he always says that he doesn't drink. But he drinks Coca-Cola and Jack Daniel's all the time. I call it his hillbilly cocktail. No. He really hates

(famous manager of a very famous rock star).

But nobody hates anybody so much as

(wife of famous manager of a very famous rock star)

hates both

(famous manager of a very famous rock star)

and

(a very famous rock star).

(Laughter)

136

(A TREND-SETTING WOMAN OF HIGH SOCIAL STANDING)

WARHOL: You know, I -- I never think -- I never think about beauties in girls, but you -- I mean, you know -- like, you know, because they're always there. But then when the next beautiful, younger girl comes along, it is scary. It's so interesting.

CAPOTE: Yeah, but they're very rare.

WARHOL: No. Well, they're very rare, but they -- they do come along, you know.

CAPOTE: I mean, I can name on one hand all the women that I have thought that were really beautiful. And at this point, none of them were what you would exactly call young. Some of them indeed are dead. I always said, of all the women I know in my life, that the person who has the most -- everything going for her was (a trend-setting woman of high social standing).

WARHOL: See, I didn't --

CAPOTE: And yet the interesting thing about (a trend-setting woman of high social standing) was that she really wasn't beautiful.

WARHOL: You see, I never knew her when she was really --

CAPOTE: She just managed to create this extraordinary illusion of it, which I thought was this, you know, it was a great work of art. It was fantastic.

WARHOL: Well, how did she do that?

CAPOTE: Makeup, clothes, her hair, everything. Actually, she had a broken nose. All the teeth in her mouth had been knocked out in a car accident.

WARHOL: Oh, no. Really?

CAPOTE: They looked false.

WARHOL: Oh. Wow.

CAPOTE: But she just managed somehow by everything she did --

WARHOL: But she didn't have -- she didn't have caps? She actually had -- she didn't have caps?

CAPOTE: She just had straight -- well, but I mean, she had all the -- she had a -- was in a big car accident.

WARHOL: When? When she was younger?

CAPOTE: Oh, when she was about 17 years old.

WARHOL: Really?

CAPOTE: That's why her nose got broken. That's how she got that pretty nose. I mean, she didn't really have that pretty nose. She got it through a car accident.

WARHOL: God.

CAPOTE: But she created -- more than any single person that I've ever known. She moved and then suddenly everything else dimmed down because she really was beautiful. She really knew how to wear something, and she was always so marvelously --

WARHOL: Who -- who's another person?

CAPOTE: A second person -- but she's no longer beautiful. But the first time I ever saw her I -- she really knocked me out. And that was in Maxine's. In 1947 this woman walks into Maxine's in this incredibly little Balenciaga suit. But with a rather large black hat -- like that -- everything. I mean, it was something to remember. And I said to Maxine, "Who is that woman?" And they said, "Oh, her name is

(another trend-setting woman of high social standing)."

That was just the name she was using. She had actually been married to one of the biggest Nazis in Germany.

WARHOL: Who was it?

CAPOTE: She had managed to escape out of Germany and -- because she became a lover of the ambassador from Spain. She then went to Paris and she married --

WARHOL: Was she --

CAPOTE: Well, she had these two children, et cetera. And she -- and she was

(famous European fashion designer)'s

greatest friend. He always said to me, "I've never designed a dress in my life that -- ever since I first saw

139

her, except for this woman, who's a Mexican." And it was (another trend-setting woman of high social standing).

WARHOL: Oh, really? Oh.

CAPOTE: Oh. But, my God, she was simply unforgettable.

WARHOL: She had a Nazi -- yeah.

CAPOTE: Oh, yes. Oh, she was one of Hitler's greatest friends. She used to give parties for Hitler all the time in Berlin.

WARHOL: I know. That's why they were who they were.

CAPOTE: Yeah, sure. I know all about it, but let's not go into it.

(another trend-setting woman of high social standing) was Hitler's greatest host. She had a fantastic house. And she would give parties for all of these -- to do -- well, doing, you know, actually, really what she's doing at this minute. She's kind of great. She's sort of bright in a way. She really is. She certainly has fantastic taste.

WARHOL: But those two women look alike. I mean, see you have a -- those two really did look alike. One was dark and one was a blond.

CAPOTE: Are you talking about --

WARHOL: Yes. They do. They have the same kind of -- they have the same face, but one -- don't they?

CAPOTE: They had as much taste, but they did not look at all --

140

WARHOL: Really? No, but -- yeah. Didn't they look alike

a little? I mean, they have the same sort of pointed --

CAPOTE: Well, all I can tell you is that I went on no less

than five yacht cruises with them, and I can tell you --

WARHOL: And that same hair -- well, I mean -- Yeah. I

know. You know them better than --

CAPOTE: First of all, they hated each other.

WARHOL: Well, the -- well, I met them both, you know -- I

met them at the same time sort of.

CAPOTE: Ah,

(a trend-setting woman of high social standing)

just despised

(another trend-setting woman of high social standing).

Because she was really mean to her. I mean, she really

was mean.

(A POWERFUL HOLLYWOOD
TALENT AGENT)

CAPOTE: Wait.

(a powerful Hollywood talent agent)

gave a dinner party for 22 people for me. It was an all-out

movie celebrity party.

WARHOL: She has everybody,

(macho male movie star),

(heartthrob male movie star),

(female child star).

She turned down

(younger male movie star).

How did she get so powerful, Truman?

CAPOTE: Oh, I can tell you the whole story backwards and forwards.

WARHOL: Oh. OK.

CAPOTE: She went out to California, she was working for -- she was working for Music Corporation of America, MCA. And she got a real big thing going there and she got a whole lot of stars. She got

(major male movie star).

She got

(famous female singer).

She really is something, that

(famous female singer).

She's always got something up her skirts. I wrote a song that she claims is her favorite song. Which is really the song that started her career. She recorded it on her first record. In interviews she always says that's her favorite song, but she doesn't do it very well. She takes every ballad and turns it into a three-act opera. That's (famous female singer)'s

great fault as a singer, as far as I'm concerned.

WARHOL: Oh. How did she get

(famous female singer)?

CAPOTE: Who knows how anybody gets anything, but, nevertheless, she did. She doesn't have everybody. Do you know her?

WARHOL: Who?

CAPOTE: Do you know . . .

(a powerful Hollywood talent agent).

WARHOL: Well, you know, we -- I don't know how we ever knew -- well, yeah.

CAPOTE: There's something about her that's amusing. She calls me up sometimes and I talk to her on the phone. She's very funny. And she tells me all kind of nutty things. She told me this extraordinary thing one day on the phone. She said that she and old

(a famous author)

and

(a famous author)'s

boyfriend -- she's

(a famous author)'s

agent -- he's the only writer that she has -- But, anyway, she was telling me this one story about how they drove down to Mexico -- just over the border. And they were in this place and they picked up this guy and they brought him back. And he was 12 inches long and as thick as your wrist. And she said, "But I was the only one that could take it."

WARHOL: Oh, really.

CAPOTE: And I said, "Well, congratulations. Every now and then somebody's got to have something going for them!"

(a powerful Hollywood talent agent)

is a total tramp.

(Laughter.)

(A LEGENDARY MOVIE STAR)

CAPOTE: I will hold forth -- my sex life with

(legendary movie star).

WARHOL: Oh, great. Really? Oh, you promise. Really. God.

CAPOTE: Well, I damn near had one.

WARHOL: Did you really?

CAPOTE: No. Except that -- I was kidding. But the thing is, you know, I was an insomniac. I'm not such an insomniac as I was, but there was a -- well, pretty much of one. But -- but

(legendary movie star)

was a real insomniac. She never went to sleep. And she, you know -- there was -- she had a list of about four or five other insomniacs that she felt it was perfectly safe to call at 4:00 o'clock in the morning or 5:00 o'clock in the morning. And she used to call me at 3:00 or 4:00 o'clock in the morning and talk for an hour and a half describing -- I mean, when she would get, you know, really down to she had nothing further to talk about. And she would tell me about the grubbiest details of her sex life in London in the '20s. And anything -- she would -- but she was an -- she was great. She was really funny. Did you know her? Well, you knew -- you met her through me, didn't you?

WARHOL: Just a little bit. Yeah.

CAPOTE: She was an extraordinary person.

WARHOL: Oh. Yeah, extraordinary.

CAPOTE: She said my favorite line ever, my favorite sort of kinky line. And everybody's got some kind of thing, but this really sets them off for no reason. I mean, it doesn't really mean anything. Well, she was telling me one day this story about how she had this house out in Kisco in 1931 or '32, or whenever. And she had one of the very first portable radios ever made. And she and

(noted English actress and movie star)

were lying out on the lawn sunning themselves with this portable radio. And suddenly, the announcer came on and says, "We have a very special announcement" and said about the Lindbergh baby being kidnapped. Early this morning, somebody on a ladder, et cetera, stole into the house, and et cetera, and stole Colonel Lindbergh and Mrs. Lindbergh's baby, et cetera. And they listened to this in long silence. And then the end of the special announcement came, and then

(noted English actress and movie star)

turned and said, "Well,

(legendary movie star)

we're well out of that one."

(Laughter.)

WARHOL: That's a really great story.

PLACES

NEW YORK

WARHOL: New York's gotten so incredible. It changes so quickly. It just changes like that. It's a whole different place. I mean, it's so incredible.

CAPOTE: No one is from Fire Island.

LONDON

WARHOL: Oh. We stayed at The Dorchester and that was really terrific.

CAPOTE: I hate it.

WARHOL: Well, no. It's just bought by the Arabs. It's great, my God.

CAPOTE: It's terrible. There's only one nice restaurant I know. Only one -- there's only one nice restaurant and there's only one nice hotel in London.

WARHOL: Which one?

CAPOTE: The Common. They have the best restaurant and they have -- it's the best hotel.

WARHOL: Well, The Dorchester was terrific. It really was terrific. And the new Barclay -- everybody says they're --

CAPOTE: But, of course, I don't like anything about London. So it doesn't matter.

WARHOL: You don't? Well, now -- really?

CAPOTE: I don't like anything about it.

WARHOL: You're kidding? Because it had changed so much now. It's a whole different -- it's different.

CAPOTE: I know London very, very well for a very long time.

WARHOL: Well, you know when it was really -- you know, when it was really --

CAPOTE: And I don't like it and I have never liked it. I mean, I love the houses and I love a lot of English people. And I love all their flowers and I love this and that.

WARHOL: Well, we had the best times, because --

CAPOTE: But it's just something about it that is so oppressive. It is the most boring place in the world.

WARHOL: Oh, no. Let -- let me tell you our -- we -- we had parties. We had --

(British hostess)

is married now, has the most beautiful house in the world. It's like a block long, because it's got this artist studio in back. And so it's like 18 little houses together. And she made it one long house, you know, behind a whole block. Well, it's just -- she -- she had it decorated -- she had a party for

(famous American folk singer).

It was so exciting.

CAPOTE: Oh. I can't stand anything about London and I have no interest in going there.

WARHOL: No, no. It was really good. I mean, you couldn't believe it. It was really good.

CAPOTE: Would you like a lot of free airplane tickets to London? Because I get them sent to me every other day by the BBC.

WARHOL: Well, I don't like to travel. I mean, I have gone three times.

(Laughter.)

CAPOTE: Free, round-trip tickets you can have from me at any time.

WARHOL: But it's on the Concorde.

CAPOTE: What?

WARHOL: Oh. The Concorde's the best. Oh, God. You leave at 8:00. You come here at 6:00. I mean, you drink on the way and you're drunk all day. And, oh, it's terrific. Three hours. It's fast. And the service is great.

CAPOTE: And then I end up in the regional hospital.

(Laughter.)

LOS ANGELES

CAPOTE: I have the most incredible collection of plane tickets.

WARHOL: Really. How great. You mean, you win prizes on these programs or --

CAPOTE: No. They give them to me.

WARHOL: They do? Really?

CAPOTE: I mean, these broadcast companies send them to me about, you know.

WARHOL: Oh.

CAPOTE: To say 15 words on some sort of thing they can tape right away. And then I say, "I'll do it if you'll send me -- " I don't want to be paid.

WARHOL: I know. I do the same thing. Yeah. I do the same thing.

CAPOTE: I don't want to be paid. I don't want to be paid, because I don't want to be paid -- pay the income tax.

WARHOL: Oh, yeah. Oh, yeah. That's a great idea.

CAPOTE: So, I say, "I'll do it if you'll send me a first class --
two first-class, round-trip tickets to -- " I have . . .

WARHOL: It's -- it's a great idea.

CAPOTE: . . . airplane tickets up to here.

WARHOL: Oh. It's a great idea. Well, you should maybe
change it for Cartier watches.

CAPOTE: Well, we can exchange tickets where you want
to go or something.

WARHOL: Okay. I'll --

CAPOTE: I mean, I have so many round-trip tickets from
Los Angeles to New York that you wouldn't even believe it.

(Laughter.)

WARHOL: Oh, great. God.

CAPOTE: I mean, I could go back and forth every day of
the week.

(Laughter.)

WARHOL: Oh, great. Oh, Truman, that's another good
story we should do. We should actually just go to Los
Angeles for lunch and come back, for dinner and come
back the same day. I wonder what -- should we do it?

CAPOTE: Well, we've got enough tickets.

WARHOL: We'll take -- yeah. We'll take -- we'll take -- it
would be great. Yeah. For a meal and then come back.
Wouldn't it be great? You leave in the morning. I mean,
it's three hours earlier. I mean --

CAPOTE: You leave at dawn.

WARHOL: It only takes five hours. And then you take the night thing back.

CAPOTE: Well, we'll just go -- we'll just go -- we'll go to La Maison.

WARHOL: Yes.

CAPOTE: For -- and have dinner. And then we'll go back to the airport for another plane. Oh, yeah. Oh. We can do it all the way.

WARHOL: Well, that would be at least a day.

CAPOTE: It will be a great joke.

WARHOL: It would be.

CAPOTE: God knows we have enough plane tickets.

(Laughter.)

STORIES

DOG

CAPOTE: . . . to this party here in New York -- and so this girl, who absolutely turned him on like no one ever had. So, she turned out to be a number one fashion model. In fact, was and is still New York's number one fashion model. But he didn't get to meet her, and he became obsessed by this whole thing about this girl, and clipping her pictures out of magazines and had quite a scrapbook, a little collective -- and he kept trying to arrange to meet her. He himself being, by the way, very intelligent, very attractive, and a most presentable person. Finally, one day, he mentioned this girl to me, and began talking about his particular obsession with her. And I said, "Well, I know somebody who knows her very well." Which indeed I did, it was a theatrical producer here in New York. So I said, "I'll call him up and see if he can't arrange a -- you know, an evening for you, a

date." So after about a month of this theatrical producer continuously talking with this girl, arranged this
date. She said, oh, well, all right, if he's so charming,
he's so attractive, et cetera, I'll go out with him. So he
was in a state of terrific excitement and he booked a
table in a very good restaurant and theater tickets and
planned to take her dancing afterwards, after supper.
So, the evening arrived, and it was a warm June evening
here in New York, unseasonably warm. This girl lived
on the Upper West 70s, in one of those great big, sort of
gothic apartment houses, those *Rosemary's Baby* kind
of buildings -- And he arrived there around 6:30, getting
towards twilight, and he went up in this creaky old elevator. Now, as you know, all those apartments have very
high ceilings, very deep, dark, very high ceilings and
sort of windows that go from the ceiling to the floor,
like French doors almost. Anyway, he rang the bell and
a cleaning woman answered the door. She said, oh, well,
the young lady was still dressing, but for him to come
on into the living room. Unfortunately, the cleaning
woman was just leaving, but just go ahead because the
young lady would be out in a minute. So, he goes into
the living room. Well, it's an enormous, big, roomy room
and all the windows are open because it was very warm.
There are four big windows, two on each side of the room.

One of these windows looks down into a deep courtyard, about 12 floors below, and there's sort of a little slight breeze stirring these curtains. So he walks in and he sees over in the corner that there's a tray, a table with drinks set out on it, and he pours himself a scotch. And he's pouring scotch, he suddenly hears this peculiar sound. This thump, thump, thump. And he looks around and there in the corner of the room is an enormous Great Dane, weighing about 250 pounds. This gigantic, small horse of a dog. And the dog had a ball between his paws and is going thump, thump, thump, thump, thump with this ball, back and forth. So my friend walks over, and he says, aha, he says, I know what you want. So he stoops down and picks up the ball and he bounces it so that it hits the ceiling and the dog jumps up, grabs it in his mouth, and rushes up to him all wimpy and giggling with happiness. So he takes the ball out of the dog's mouth, and there's opposite of him this great empty wall with no pictures on it or anything. So he takes the ball and he thumps it up against the wall, like this. Well, the ball hits the wall and skids and it goes out the window and so does the dog. When he rushes to the window, and down, down, down, down, splash. In exactly this moment, the young lady comes rushing into the room veiled in perfume and chatter. Saying to him, oh, I'm so sorry I'm so late. We'll have to hurry or we won't be able to go to dinner and the theater, and et cetera. She's bubbling, bubbling, bubbling. He's absolutely paralyzed. He just stands -- He can't even say hello, how are you. And he's -- what's he going to do? Is he going to say to her your dog just jumped out the window? Well, if he says to her your dog just jumped out the window, that means the end of their evening. On the other hand, if he doesn't tell her, well, what's going to happen? So as he's in this great moral dilemma standing there, the girl keeps on moving him along towards the elevator towards the door, hurrying him, saying, oh, I'm so sorry, we've got to hurry, a blah, blah, blah, a blah, blah, blah. So they get downstairs and they get in a taxi. Well, she keeps trying to make conversation with him, and he just keeps looking at her, as though he's going to burst into tears any moment. And she's getting quite confused. I mean, what is this? Why did this guy take me out on this date? What's it all about? So they get to the restaurant, and they order the meal. And so during the course of the meal -- which he can't eat, he's just picking around -- she says to him, oh, did you see my dog when you were there this evening? And he says, yes, I -- I -- I saw your dog. So she then proceeds to tell him that she's had this dog since she was 16 years old. And he is the closest, dearest thing in her life, her guardian, her best friend. And that if she didn't have that dog, her family would never have let her come to New York to be a model in the first place, and on and on. And so suddenly he gets up and he goes to the men's room and throws up. So then they go to the theater, and it's absolute agony, he can't sit through the thing. He has to keep getting up and walking up and down in the back aisle. And he's really -- and he's pouring sweat. Doesn't know what he's going to do. He knows that he can't go on with this evening much longer. So when the play ends, he says to her, you know, I really wanted to take you dancing after supper but because I have this virus and I've really been feeling very ill for the past couple of days, do you mind if I take you home? And she says, I do mind if you take me home, she says, because I don't want to go home with you. She says, I don't know what this is all about, she says, but I mean after all this great campaign to take me out, she says, you've been treating me all evening like I was a pariah. And so she walks off and gets in a cab, slams the door, and leaves him. Okay. He gets in a cab, he goes home, goes upstairs and gets in bed. He's feeling very, very, very bad. He's really ruined the whole thing. And he keeps thinking, well, what could he have done, what should he have done. So, finally, he calls the producer, who had arranged the date with the girl, and he tells him the entire story of what happened. And he asked him, what should I have done? What could I have done that was different? And the producer says to him, well, you remember when you were in the restaurant? And he said, yes. And do you remember when she asked you if you had seen the dog that evening? And he says, yes. He says, well, what you should have said was, yes, I saw him, and I must say he looked awfully depressed.

Well, that really happened. And I thought about writing it many, many times, but then I decided that it wasn't really my kind of story. I mean, I enjoyed it for its narrative value, but it was more like a Saki short story, something that Saki might have written, or John Collier, or even O. Henry for that matter. But it wasn't my particular kind of story because I felt it was very anecdotal and that any number of writers could write it and perhaps a great deal better than me. My sort of criteria and about what I choose to write is, is this really my material?

Is this something that belongs entirely to me or can I imagine someone else writing this particular book or story? If after a while I decide that I can't imagine someone else writing it, it becomes a great pressure on me. And I -- and, finally, that's how I choose my material or, rather, my material chooses me.

MECHANIC

CAPOTE: Did you ever know

(noted Broadway producer)?

WARHOL: I did, yeah.

CAPOTE: Okay. Anyway, he was a Broadway producer, who now has moved to San Francisco. He made a lot of money. He produced all the

(famous playwright)

plays, but he was better than that. He had a lot of style and he made a lot of money. He bought this beautiful house in Telegraph Hill. But my favorite thing I ever remember about

(noted Broadway producer)

was in 1952 or '53. Remember when those -- the very first of those Mercedes, the brown Mercedes convertibles came out? The two -- the four-seater? I knew about it and talked about it. Well, he bought one. He hadn't driven anywhere, and he finally decided he was going to give it a little run. And he has this old mother, who was living in Miami, so he decided to give it a little old run down to Miami, to see old mommy. And two days of that was enough and he had to turn back. He was driving through North Carolina and it was getting dusk, it was getting really dark. It was getting dark. So he thought, there was a gas station coming up, and he thought, well, I better get some gas here and I'll ask where is the best, nearest motel. So he pulls into this garage and this really very attractive, good-looking young guy comes out, and he says to him, fill it up, you know. And he goes to the men's room and he comes back, he has the keys to the car in his hand. And he walks back and he's taking a really total picture of this scene. And he says to this guy, he says, where's the nearest motel that's really good? The guy says to him, about a mile up the road. Then the guy says to him, what kind of a car is this, anyway? He said, I never saw a car like this. And

(noted Broadway producer)

says, it's a Mercedes convertible. And he told him, this guy, I never saw a car like this. He says, you know, I'd just about give anything in the world to have a car like that.

(noted Broadway producer)

says to him, oh, would you really? I mean, would you really give anything in the world? He says, yeah. He says, I haven't seen anything like it. I mean, that's the most beautiful thing I've ever seen. So

(noted Broadway producer)

has the keys to the car and he says to the guy, he says,

hold up your hand. He says, now catch. He threw the keys at the guy and he caught the keys in his hand. And

(noted Broadway producer)

said, it's very simple, I mean, you really want that car, you got it. And the guy started to laugh, he says, what are you -- what kind of joke is this? What kind of -- He says, nah. He says, if you will drive me to Washington, DC, in the morning and I can take a plane to New York, you can have the car. He says, there's just one little thing about it. And the guy says, what? And

(noted Broadway producer)

says, what time do you close? And the guy says, what do you mean? He says, well, that motel's one mile down the road, what time do you close? Because you're going to have to spend the night with me and then drive me. And the guy said to him, right now? And closed the garage, and you know what happened?

WARHOL: No. What?

CAPOTE: He went there and he not only spent the night with

(noted Broadway producer),

he came on to New York with him, and he lived with him for five years.

GLOSSARY

(In the order they occur in the text).

STUDIO 54

A very popular disco in NYC in the late 1970s. Crowds of people tried to gain entry every night. Celebrities, sex, and drugs were all in great supply.

HALSTON

A famous designer of women's clothing in the 1970s. Designed Jackie Kennedy's famous pillbox hat.

LIZA MINNELLI

Tony- and Academy Award–winning actress. Star of the films *Cabaret* and *Arthur*. A celebrated singer, she is the daughter of Judy Garland and film director Vincent Minnelli.

GLOSSARY

MARTIN SCORSESE

Academy Award–winning director of *Taxi Driver*, *Mean Streets*, *Goodfellas*, and *Casino*, along with the infamous bomb *New York, New York*, starring Liza Minnelli and Robert De Niro. Martin also directed Liza's Broadway show *The Act*.

ROBERT DE NIRO

Academy Award–winning actor. Starred in many films directed by Martin Scorsese, including *Taxi Driver*. Also known for his role in *The Godfather, Part II*.

JACK HALEY

Andy was actually referring to Jack Haley Jr., who was married to Liza Minnelli in the 1970s. Jack was a writer and producer and the son of actor Jack Haley, best known for his beloved performance as the Tin Man in the classic *Wizard of Oz*.

MIKHAIL BARYSHNIKOV

World-famous ballet dancer who defected from the Soviet Union to the United States.

MADISON SQUARE GARDEN

Known as "the world's most famous arena," it is located in the center of New York City and has featured concerts

with the biggest musicians in the world including Frank
Sinatra, Elvis Presley, Led Zeppelin, the Rolling Stones,
David Bowie, and Elton John.

ELTON JOHN
Pop star who became the most famous musician on Earth
in the early to mid-1970s with a string of number one
albums. Elton wore outrageous costumes and eyeglasses
onstage and did tend to be a bit overweight at times.

DAVID BOWIE
Came to fame as a glam rocker. His first number one single
was called "Space Oddity." Bowie went on to have a successful career in various styles of music. He was never as
popular as Elton or the Rolling Stones.

ROLLING STONES
One of the most famous and popular rock and roll bands
of all time. Came to fame in the mid-1960s and went on to
become one of the biggest live attractions in music history.

MICK JAGGER
Lead singer of the Rolling Stones, and a major star in his
own right. Mick asked Andy Warhol to design the covers
of two Stones albums, *Sticky Fingers* and *Love You Live*.

GLOSSARY

FRED ASTAIRE

Movie star and extraordinary dancer.

LA PETITE MARMITE

Exclusive restaurant, frequented by high society in Manhattan in the 1970s.

C. Z. GUEST

An American socialite. She was known for being a horseback rider and gardener. Her daughter, Cornelia, was a friend of Andy's in the early '80s.

ALLAN CARR

Producer of the film *Grease*, and the Broadway hit musical *La Cage aux Folles*. Known for his outrageous and excessive parties in Hollywood. Also for wearing caftans studded with diamonds.

TENNESSEE WILLIAMS

Famous playwright of *The Glass Menagerie*, *A Streetcar Named Desire*, and *Summer and Smoke*. By the mid-1970s he was also well known for public drunkenness and outrageous public behavior.

GLOSSARY

THE NEW YORK TIMES MAGAZINE
Magazine published every Sunday by the *New York Times*. Featured a two-part story on Truman in 1978 that claimed he broke up marriages by "stealing" husbands. The article noted Truman's troubles with drugs and alcohol.

LINDBERGH'S BABY
This refers to the kidnapping and death of Charles Lindbergh's baby. Lindbergh was a well-known aviator. His twenty-month-old son, Charles Jr., was taken from the Lindbergh home in New Jersey, while both parents were at home, in 1932. The body of the child was eventually discovered, with a head wound found to be the cause of death. The kidnapping was national news, with many ransom notes and secret meetings. Eventually Bruno Richard Hauptmann was tried and executed for the crime.

ANSWERED PRAYERS
Truman's unfinished novel, four chapters of which were serialized in *Esquire*. One of these chapters, "La Cote Basque," detailed secrets of Truman's society friends. They very quickly shunned him, adding to his swift decline and death. The chapters were eventually published in book form. It remains an open question whether Truman ever

finished writing the novel, as he claims he had. The complete novel has never been found.

ESQUIRE

The magazine that published Truman's advance chapters from *Answered Prayers*.

FOREST LAWN CEMETERY

Famous cemetery in Los Angeles, where many celebrities are buried or interred.

MARILYN MONROE

Famous movie star and pinup girl. Had an affair with John F. Kennedy. Later married to playwright Arthur Miller. Died after taking an overdose of sleeping pills.

TAB

A popular diet cola in the 1970s. Served in a pink can.

JACKIE KENNEDY

First Lady of the United States when married to John F. Kennedy. Was in the open car when Kennedy was assassinated. Later married oil tycoon and billionaire Aristotle Onassis. Was the most famous woman in the world for a time. Hounded by paparazzi.

JOHN F. "JACK" KENNEDY

President of the United States. Was assassinated by Lee Harvey Oswald in Dallas, Texas. Notorious playboy.

WHITE HOUSE

The official residence of the president of the United States and First Lady while in office. Located in Washington, D.C.

POLAROID

A type of film and camera. The photographs are ejected from the camera and develop instantly. There were different camera models and different types of film. Andy famously used Polaroid photos as the basis for his society portraits.

HAZELDEN

One of the early addiction treatment centers in the United States. Located in Minnesota.

12 STEPS

The path to addiction recovery as practiced by Alcoholics Anonymous.

AA

The commonly used abbreviation for Alcoholics Anonymous.

GLOSSARY

ELAINE'S

Famous Upper East Side restaurant, frequented by high society and celebrities in New York City in the 1970s. Run by Elaine Kaufman.

HUMPHREY BOGART (BOGIE)

Star of *The Maltese Falcon, The African Queen*, and *Casablanca*. Had a reputation for being a "man's man." Was married to actress Lauren Bacall.

BEAT THE DEVIL

Movie directed by John Huston and written by Truman Capote and John Huston. Shot in Italy. Released in 1953.

JACK DUNPHY

Playwright, author, former dancer, and longtime companion of Truman Capote.

JOAN MCCRACKEN

Gained fame as "the girl who falls down" in the original Broadway musical *Oklahoma!* She went on to dance in other Broadway shows and in films.

GLOSSARY

OKLAHOMA!

Groundbreaking 1943 Broadway musical written by Rodgers and Hammerstein and choreographed by Agnes de Mille.

BOB FOSSE

Famous dancer turned choreographer and director. Created the musicals *Chicago*, *Pippin*, *Dancin'*, and *Sweet Charity*. Directed semiautobiographical film *All That Jazz*, as well as the Academy Award–winning *Cabaret*.

U.N. PLAZA

One of the first new luxury apartment buildings in Manhattan. Truman's apartment was on the twenty-second floor overlooking the East River.

VALERIE SOLANAS

Radical lesbian playwright, author of *S.C.U.M. Manifesto*. Was angry that Andy didn't respond to her play, and so shot him at point-blank range. Andy barely survived.

THE FACTORY

Sometimes referred to as the Silver Factory. This was Andy's famous studio located on East Forty-Seventh Street. The walls were covered in aluminum foil. The scene of many parties and film shoots. And where Andy created some of his most iconic paintings.

CAMPBELL'S SOUP CANS
Andy's first famous paintings. A series of thirty-two canvases, they were first shown in Los Angeles in 1962, where only five of the paintings were initially sold by dealer Irving Blum. The critical reception to Andy's first solo show of Pop Art was unkind. Blum eventually reacquired the five paintings to keep the set together, which he then purchased himself.

NEW YORK POST
One of New York City's daily newspapers. Known for lurid covers and coverage of celebrity gossip.

MY DECADE WITH
ANDY AND TRUMAN

ROB ROTH

I began work on *WARHOLCAPOTE* in 2007. It has been a long ride filled with both joyous and difficult emotions. I sometimes wonder, if I had known what it was going to take, would I have started this whole process? Honestly, the answer is that I didn't really have a choice.

This all started with a phone call from my friend Rosie O'Donnell. Ro invited me and my then boyfriend, now husband, Patrick, to go on a gay family cruise. I initially declined. The thought of being on a boat for a week filled me with dread, and the idea of being surrounded by children was the clincher—but Patrick thought it would be a great place for him to cram for his medical board exams. Being the good boyfriend I attempted to be, I called Ro back and accepted her offer. In reality, though, I was dreading this sea voyage. What was I going to do trapped on a boat for a week?

AFTERWORD

I purchased a brand-new copy of *The Andy Warhol Diaries*, edited by Pat Hackett, one of my all-time favorite books. I'd read it many times before, it is always a joy to return to, and I thought it would keep me safely occupied in my stateroom, far away from the children.

Which it did. I was fairly far along in the book when I came across this entry:

THURSDAY, JUNE 29, 1978
"I told Truman I would tape him and we could write a Play-A-Day . . ."

and then:

WEDNESDAY, JULY 5, 1978
". . . Gee, Truman, can't I just tape you, the real thing, and do plays about real people?"

and, finally, in a conversation with Elizabeth Taylor:

SATURDAY, OCTOBER 28, 1978
". . . I want you to play Truman Capote for me on Broadway."

Tapes? A play? Broadway? In all the many times I had read *The Diaries*, I had never picked up on these tidbits. I knew Andy had an obsession with Broadway. There was even a plan to have a robot-Andy perform selections from his *Philosophy* book as a Broadway show. As I continued reading, I came across this later entry:

SUNDAY, DECEMBER 15, 1985
"I got up and read the transcripts of those days with Truman that I'd taped . . . but by talking in them so much myself, I ruined them. I should've just kept my mouth shut."

Now I was really intrigued. Did these tapes actually exist? Where were they? How far did they get with this project? Did a script exist from the tapes? Did Andy talk so much he actually ruined them? By the time Patrick and I got off the ship, I was obsessed.

When we got back to New York City I called my friend Vincent Fremont, who was Andy's right-hand man for many years. Did he know anything about these tapes? Vincent recalled Andy and Truman talking about writing a Broadway play together, but he had no idea if they actually recorded anything. He suggested that I speak with the head archivist at the Warhol Museum in Pittsburgh, Matt Wrbican. Matt said that the museum had a trove of cassette recordings—over three thousand—but that they were under lock and key and inaccessible to anyone until 2037, fifty years after Andy's death. He said that I would need the permission of the board of The Andy

Warhol Foundation for the Visual Arts in order to access the tapes.

The president of the board, Joel Wachs, told me that when Andy died, the board didn't know what to do with his large collection of tapes, as he recorded many of them surreptitiously, which was illegal at the time. The foundation lawyers decided that they would put a fifty-year embargo on the recordings, and let lawyers decide what to do with them at that time. My Andy and Truman adventure was over before it started.

I moped. And in my wallowing, I realized something: Truman knew he was being recorded! Perhaps this changed things. I called Joel and explained my position. He agreed to go back to the board and see if this changed things at all. Luckily for me, the artist Cindy Sherman and filmmaker John Waters were on the Warhol board, and apparently were insistent that I be allowed access to the recordings. They, along with Joel, persuaded the lawyers to draft a deal memo, which required me to indemnify the foundation and pay for all costs associated with locating, digitizing, and transcribing any cassettes that were found with some sort of notation indicating that Truman was on the tape.

I was elated. The hunt for the tapes could begin.

Matt Wrbican now had permission to unseal the stored tapes and look at each one individually to ascertain whether Truman was on it. Matt found fifty-nine ninety-minute cassettes with "Truman" in Andy's handwriting. I had these tapes digitally transferred, and then had the digital files transcribed by a bonded court reporting company. This meant that the company legally stood behind the transcriptions, and that they were extremely accurate, capturing every sound that was on each tape. This was very expensive, but I took the plunge.

The transcriptions and digital recordings arrived slowly, over a period of approximately nine months. The tapes themselves were not dated, and they arrived in no particular order. The day the first one arrived I eagerly sat down with my headphones on, and with the transcript open in front of me, so I could read along. It was not what I was expecting at all. Rather than Andy and Truman sitting down and talking about a play, this tape had them together somewhere in Texas. Attending an event at someone's home. Then going to an antique store. Then driving back to their hotel. There were many voices on the tape. Most unidentifiable. I didn't find even one sentence about a play. My heart sank.

The next tape took two weeks to arrive. The waiting was making me anxious as hell. I decided that I wouldn't listen to the tapes one at a time. Instead, I waited for the remaining fifty-eight digital audio files and printed transcripts to arrive. Then I could do a deep dive into the materials, uninterrupted.

The second tape was a recording of a lunch with four people. Mostly Andy and Truman talking to each other. Lots of funny gossip about others, some famous people, others I didn't know. Still nothing that made me think of a play. I did laugh out loud a few times. It was clear they were good friends and enjoyed each other's company. It was really incredible to be a fly on the wall at this private lunch, so to speak. I made an index of what they talked about on each tape. This went on for a few more cassettes, lots of fun gossip, talk about current plays and movies.

And then I arrived at the magic tape.

Andy said, "We should work together." And they proceeded to discuss working on a Broadway play, which Andy suggested should be based on their taped conversations. The hair on my arms stood up. Here was the concept for the play in their own words. Andy and Truman told me what to do. Take their words and make a play out of them. A play that would be both real and imagined. I realized that this idea was something they had each explored in their own art. Andy, for example, took a real photograph of Marilyn Monroe and filtered it through his imagination—the outcome was the Marilyn paintings known the world over. Truman took the true story of the Clutter family murder, filtering it through his imagination to create *In Cold Blood*. They were telling me to do the same.

To say I was elated is an understatement. But I also realized that I had a serious responsibility now. I was going to create imagined conversations utilizing only their words. The words I chose, and how I ordered them, were going to paint a portrait of these two geniuses. Did I want to reinforce the popular sense of who they were? Or reveal their true selves? I thought that Truman would want his true self revealed, and that Andy would loathe that. I realized I didn't have to decide anything until I had finished listening to the recordings. Surely there would be more clues for me as I proceeded.

I continued to bask in the unreality of actually listening to these two heroes of mine in private conversation. Andy and Truman had been a part of my life since I was a preteen. My parents took me to the Museum of Modern Art when I was nine and bought me a postcard of Andy's *Flowers*. I just loved these paintings. They were kind of like cartoons. I could see it was a flower, but a very abstract, imaginative flower. At least to my nine-year-old eye. I was a nerd, spending many hours in our town library poring over books. I liked researching things. I began to study Andy, who was just so fascinating to my child-self. His odd, alien look, his Silver Factory with the tinfoil walls.

AFTERWORD

As I got a little older I began noticing Andy in the paper, partying at Studio 54, attending film premieres. He seemed glamorous. And he seemed gay to me. I knew that I was gay when I was ten. I was troubled by this, but made a decision: I would just deal with this when I was eighteen. Maybe it was a phase. But suspecting Andy was gay and seeing his fabulous life made me feel better.

Truman came into my life around the same time as Andy. My parents weren't voracious readers, but they had many bestsellers on our bookshelf in the den. I could read at a young age, and when they were out, would take books off the shelf. Particularly *The Godfather* and *Valley of the Dolls*, which had very racy sections that made my little heart beat faster. One day I pulled the hardcover of *In Cold Blood* off the shelf. I started reading and was immediately plunged into the story. When my parents came home I was still reading. They were a bit alarmed and asked if I was scared. I told them I wasn't, that it was the best book I had ever read, and to please leave me alone so I could keep reading. It took me awhile to finish, but when I did, I began researching the murders myself. At the library, I found the *New York Times* article that inspired Truman. I learned how to use the microfilm reader to find interviews with Truman from the time when he published the book. I learned about his Black and White Ball. Then one night my dad told me that Truman was going to be on Johnny Carson, and that I could stay up to watch. This might have been the first time I heard Truman speak. He was so odd! That voice! On this show he was talking about a new short novel called *Handcarved Coffins*, which my dad agreed to go out and buy the next day. I remember Truman as being fairly outrageous. And clearly gay. I just loved him.

Of the fifty-nine recordings, approximately ten featured Andy and Truman alone. This was where I started to find the most emotional material for the play. Where they talked about loneliness and fame and drugs and art. Listening to this very personal type of conversation was thrilling, but also heartbreaking. Here were two of my idols, among the most famous and successful people on Earth, and they were broken. Already I knew that the play would need to be structured to build to this kind of conversation. I knew as I was listening that their words could be fashioned into a funny and emotional play. If I could figure out the puzzle.

Using the recordings and transcripts, I took detailed notes on the content of each tape. I then repeated this process, this time highlighting sections of the transcripts that seemed "play-worthy." I called these sections "hunks," of which there were 222. A hunk could be one or two lines, or five pages of conversation. Since I only had the rights to Andy's and Truman's words, I edited the hunks so that only their words remained. I then titled each hunk: "Sex," "Studio 54," "Liza," "Writing," etc. I put each of these titles on four-by-six index cards. I then went through and graded the cards. "A" meant "this must be in the play," "B" indicated "probably will include," and the "C" cards might be useful for linking sections together.

I then began to assemble the cards in a running order. I did this over and over and over until I arrived at what I thought could be a good structure for the play. Using the cards as my guide, I put together a first rough draft.

I knew I wanted the play to move from light and funny to dark and personal. I had to choose where to set each scene, to give these conversations a backdrop and context. I decided to start at the place everyone would expect them to meet, Studio 54. Where they would naturally talk about the crowd, Liza, and other celebrities—and the conversations showed that they were funny, had a rapport, that they clearly had a friendship. I knew that the middle section of the play would take place around Truman leaving for Hazelden and rehab. Once I had the hunks arranged in an order I liked, I had to find linking material that would make this imagined conversation feel natural. This was somehow easier than I thought it would be, as the transcripts seemed to offer up natural links. The hunk outline cards were a great help here. I felt ready to have a first reading.

The first reading took place in New York City and featured Marc Wolf as Andy and Darrell Hammond as Truman. As a director, any performance comes with a fair amount of nervousness on my part. But in this case I was *also* the author.

As soon as we started, I could sense that the small audience was hanging on their every word. And they laughed a fair amount as well. But the play was too long and unbalanced. Truman was verbose and Andy was succinct. Afterward I met with Michael Eisner (the former CEO of Disney and a longtime mentor of mine; Michael gave me the unbelievable opportunity to direct Disney's first Broadway show, *Beauty and the Beast*, at my suggestion that Disney produce a Broadway show). Michael agreed that the play felt unbalanced and asked if there was more Andy to mine from the tapes. Honestly, there wasn't that much more interesting material that I hadn't used. Michael explained that anything you say in an interview is your personal copyright, so I made the request to The Warhol Foundation and Capote Literary Trust. They granted their permissions. I could use outside direct quotes from Andy and Truman. Fantastic!

I gave myself six months for additional research. I had a fairly large library of Warhol and Capote books, and now began a serious hunt for interviews. What I found amazed me. Many of the subjects that they spoke about in their private conversation on the tapes they had also spoken about in separate interviews. I found plenty of great material that fit easily into the play. I formed a bible of quotes and set about making the play feel more balanced. I decided to write a prologue in which Andy and Truman spoke about each other, using preexisting material from their separate interviews. This allowed me to give the audience the background story of how they first met, and how Andy stalked Truman. This seemed to work well on the page and made me feel that maybe I should find material for an epilogue to serve as a postscript to their relationship.

The Capote Literary Trust asked that I hold the second reading in Los Angeles. I worried that it would be hard to get people to attend a play reading out there. So, I asked Michael and Jane Eisner if they would host the reading at their home in Bel Air. We fit ninety people in their living room on a beautiful spring night. For this reading Darrell repeated his performance as Truman, and I asked Roger Bart to read Andy.

The reading went over amazingly well. Roger and Darrell found laughs that I didn't even know were there. And the laughter made the emotional parts of the play deeper. We got a rousing standing ovation, and I was surrounded by many people I did not know telling me how amazing the play was. In a post-reading discussion in the now-empty living room, Michael had notes, as he always did. The biggest note was that he thought the play should be performed without an intermission. I liked that the intermission coincided with Truman going to rehab, but at the same time I was aware that I always enjoy plays more when I see the sign in the lobby saying, "This play is performed without an intermission." I told Michael I would try it.

When I got back to New York, I looked for a way to link the two acts together sans intermission. I showed the new draft to Michael, who was very pleased and said that he wanted to produce the play on Broadway. This was a dream come true for me. I loved working with Michael, and he wanted to produce the play himself, so there wasn't going to be the endless search for investors that can come with putting a show on Broadway.

Sadly, this was not to be. Between the two foundations, Michael, and myself, we couldn't come to an agreement. I begged Michael to reconsider, but he would not. So, I was without a producer and deeply hurt.

I won't go into all the details of the struggle to find the right producer. Just that I ended up with the right ones for the play. Craig Kallman (CEO of Atlantic Records), Danny Cohen (president of Access Entertainment), Randy

Weiner (of Remarkable), and Marty Tudor (of BASE Entertainment) are a dream team. Smart, focused, and reliable. They asked me to do another reading so they could hear the play out loud.

This third reading was a real game changer. Once again Darrell and Roger played Truman and Andy. We had scheduled the reading for two days after the 2016 presidential election. It seemed clear that Hillary Clinton would win. When this didn't happen, New York City was thrown into a dark, unreal state. Yet, in this climate, we did the reading. Things got off to a good start, with Darrell and Roger getting plenty of laughs at the top. Then, as the play turned darker, the audience seemed to go with it. But then both the audience and the actors stayed in this dark place, and the play flattened out. It got slow and serious. This was not how we had rehearsed it, but it seemed that once the play turned dark the actors couldn't bring it back to a lighter track. Watching something you've directed is a strange experience, because things are totally out of your control. And if you are a director you are likely a control freak, as I am. When things start to go south and you can do nothing about it, you feel something like panic. I instinctively turned to say something to Michael Eisner, and he wasn't there. I realized in a giant bolt of clarity that I was on my

own. I needed another creative partner, a shocking revelation to have at this late stage.

Following the reading I went to dinner with Craig,
Danny, and Randy, who agreed it had not gone well. The
play wasn't as funny or moving as it read. Randy asked if
I would consider bringing on a dramaturg or even a director. I was in shock about how things had gone. I felt like
a failure. That I had let the team down in some way. They
were very supportive, and actually had the good news that
Diane Borger, the executive producer of the American Repertory Theater, was at the reading, and that they wanted
to produce the play. Which should have made me overjoyed,
but I was too shaken. (I was indeed overjoyed about this a
few days later.) Randy could see that I was very emotional
and didn't push me to make any decision. He just said that
they would support me, whatever I decided to do. When I
got home I just blurted out to Patrick, "I think I'm not
going to direct this." And he looked at me and said, "Yes."

We talked for a couple of hours. Patrick, who I call "the
human Google," did some research and found that very few
writers direct their own plays. It is much more common
in film and television, and we realized that in those disci-
plines the writer/director has a director of photography at
his side while shooting, and an editor in postproduction.

He is surrounded by creative partners during the entire process. Not so in the theater. I emailed the producers and told them I wanted to find a director. It was, perhaps, the most important decision I made.

I met with Diane Borger, the executive producer at A.R.T., who liked the reading way more than I did. She found it very moving. She thought it was smart of me to bring in a director, and we had a long talk about who we should ask. We made a list, but at the top of mine was Michael Mayer, who won the Tony Award for his *Spring Awakening* in addition to directing *Thoroughly Modern Millie* and *Hedwig and the Angry Inch*, among others. I've always enjoyed the fluidity of his directing. More importantly, we had met more than ten years prior, when we agreed to share a car and driver to attend a benefit in Ithaca, New York. A very dangerous decision, looking back on it, as eight hours in a car with someone you don't care for is a living hell; happily, we got along splendidly, and had a long talk about directing, about the isolation we both sometimes felt. So, I sent Michael an email and the play. He wrote back very quickly to say that he was incredibly busy but loved the play. We agreed to meet for lunch, where I was immediately reminded why I had liked him so much: smart as a whip, eccentric, funny, sure of his opinions.

AFTERWORD

We talked about the play, and I confessed a giant fear: What was going to happen when I sat in the theater to watch run-throughs and previews? Would I only know how to take notes as a director? Michael said, "Yes, of course you'll take notes like a director, you are a director." I burst into tears. I was so relieved. Michael wasn't threatened. He welcomed my notes. I could be myself. And he was true to his word in every way as we moved forward.

But we still needed our Andy and Truman.

Michael and our casting director, Jim Carnahan, had many fantastic ideas. Ultimately, we asked Stephen Spinella to play Andy and Leslie Jordan to play Truman. Rehearsals began in New York City, and having such amazing actors under Michael's direction was really exciting. I actually enjoyed not being the director. I let go a bit and opened my ears to their suggestions. Michael's open attitude in the rehearsal room benefited the play enormously. Under Michael's direction, I made small cuts for clarity suggested by the actors; I split one scene into two separate ones. Every day brought new ideas and questions, and I spent each night going over the things we had discussed and discovered that day, returning in the morning with fresh pages. I don't think Michael was expecting me to respond so positively or swiftly. We developed a wonderful working relationship, one of the highlights of my time working in the theater.

189

Working with Stephen and Leslie was also quite fascinating. I enjoyed watching them build up layers to their performances. Michael was less concerned about creating an imitation of Andy and Truman and more with the truth of their relationship. Stephen was incredibly inquisitive, always diving deeper into the material. He was able to try different versions of the text every time we ran through it, until he and Michael settled on what was right. Leslie's comic timing was of course incredible, and then watching him reveal the sadness inside Truman was astonishing. Michael made many strong suggestions on the text of the play, and I made many minor, and a few major, changes during the rehearsals. All was going very well. An easy, fun, and satisfying rehearsal period.

We moved to Cambridge, where the designers were overseeing the load-in of the set. It really was slightly unbelievable to see all the pieces come together at last, after ten years of work. We were in the middle of tech rehearsals when Michael and I were called down to Leslie's dressing room. Leslie was at his dressing table, crying. He had a personal emergency and had to withdraw. I couldn't quite believe what I was hearing. Of course, I was very troubled for Leslie personally. But we were a week away from our first preview. I just thought the whole thing would be canceled. Leslie asked if there was anything he could do to help. Michael asked if he could stay a day or two so that we could continue the tech rehearsals while we searched for a replacement. Leslie said of course, and after some more crying and hugs, we went upstairs and continued the tech, while Michael got on the phone with Jim Carnahan to talk about a replacement.

Jim is a casting genius, clearly, and he had a great idea. Dan Butler had appeared many times on Broadway, had played at the A.R.T., and was known for his role on *Frasier* as the straight sportscaster dude. Dan lived in Vermont, not far from the A.R.T. He was available. Michael got him on the phone while I sent him the latest script via email. He called back two hours later and said he would arrive the next day with his cat. Unbelievable!

There is nothing quite like a first preview. You feel that you have a good idea of how and where the audience will respond, but the truth is, you don't really know until it happens. There is something magical and unexplainable that happens between a live audience and live actors. When things are working as they should, a web of imagination is spun around the audience, trapping them.

I sat in the back row, my heart racing. This night was ten years in the making. Michael went up and made a short speech about our new actor, and that he would be on book for that night's performance. The audience applauded warmly. I think it's fun for an audience to be at something out of the ordinary. The houselights went down. Steve Reich music came blasting out of the speakers, and we were off . . .

The lights came up on Andy. The audience laughed at the sight of Stephen as Andy. Dan got a huge laugh from turning around and revealing himself as Truman in his chair. The audience was with the actors. As the play went on and turned darker, the audience went with it. You could hear a pin drop. They hung on every word. I found I was holding my breath for most of the first scene, and then I just relaxed. It was actually enjoyable for me to watch the performance. It had taken so long to get to this first public preview. I can remember sitting there thinking, *This is actually happening. And the audience is enjoying it.* It felt good. Very good.

The audience gave the actors a standing ovation at the curtain call. I was so emotional, shaking a little and teary, too. Michael Mayer came over to me, concerned that I was upset. "No," I said, "they're tears of relief and happiness."

I went back to New York for ten days and returned to see the final week or so of performances. Members of The Andy Warhol Foundation and Capote Literary Trust came to those shows and they were very happy with the play. I felt very proud of what we all created together. There were more than a few times during the long development process of the play when I thought it would never actually happen. Many times, in fact. I feel so fortunate to have had this opportunity to collaborate with Andy and Truman and bring their words out to the world. I hope they would be pleased.

—Rob Roth
Fire Island
May 2022

ACKNOWLEDGMENTS

The outpouring of encouragement, enthusiasm, and love shown to me by a truly remarkable group of friends has been the fuel that kept me going on the long journey of the play.

This play could never have come into being without the incredible support I received from Joel Wachs, president, Michael Dayton Hermann, and KC Maurer at The Andy Warhol Foundation for the Visual Arts, Inc., as well as Alan U. Schwartz, executor of the Truman Capote Literary Trust. Much respect and appreciation for the late Matt Wrbican, archivist at the Andy Warhol Museum in Pittsburgh, for his dedication in searching the archives to locate the actual cassette tapes that Andy recorded with Truman.

A special thanks to Jonathan Karp, publisher, and my incredible team of editors, Zachary Knoll, Ira Silverberg, Stuart Roberts and Awura Ama Barnie-Duah at Simon & Schuster. You have made this entire process fun and enjoyable.

ACKNOWLEDGMENTS

With thanks to: Kevin Adams, American Repertory Theater staff and crew, Sherri Anderson, Erika Bailey, Roger Bart, Tom Bennett, Gaetane Bertol, Len Blavatnik, Alexandre Bleau, Diane Borger, Dan Butler, Jim Carnahan, Danny Cohen, Alice Cooper, Sheryl Cooper, Jake Courtois, Emily Cuerdon, Tess Duran, Turk Edwards, Jane Eisner, Michael Eisner, Karen Evanouskas, Danny Francis, Shelly Fremont, Vincent Fremont, David Furnish, Larry Gagosian, David Geffen, Christopher Gilmore, Blake Gopnik, Shep Gordon, John Gromada, Darrell Hammond, Dave Horowitz, Elton John, Cookie Jordan, Leslie Jordan, Craig Kallman, Isabel Kallman, Charles G. LaPointe, Sam Lerner, Alta Lewis-Millard, Annabeth Lucas, Aaron Lustbader, Darrel Maloney, Michael Mayer, Terrence McCrossan, Doc McGhee, Johanna McKeon, Brian McMullen, Stanley A. Meyer, Janice Miller, Kim Miller, Steve Miller, Rosie O'Donnell, Rick Pappas, DC Parmet, Diane Paulus, Diane Quinn, Adam Rabalais, Clint Ramos, Glenn Rice, Cherie Roth, Dylan Roth, Martin Roth, Matt Roth, Phyllis Roth, Mark Shacket, Thomas Schumacher, Gene Simmons, Stephen Spinella, Paul Stanley, Rick Steiger, Christopher Vergara, Brian Webb, Randy Weiner, Matt West, Marc Wolf, Linda Woolverton, Adam Zoia, and Elizabeth Zoia.

ABOUT THE AUTHOR

ROB ROTH was nominated for a Tony Award for Best Director for his Broadway debut, *Disney's Beauty and the Beast*, which premiered in 1994, becoming one of the top ten longest-running shows in Broadway history. Rob went on to direct the show all over the world, where it has won many awards, including the Olivier Award for Best Musical in London. *Beauty* has been seen by over forty-four million people worldwide. Rob went on to direct the world premiere of *Elaborate Lives: The Legend of Aida*, collaborating with Sir Elton John and Sir Tim Rice. Rob directed the Broadway musical *Lestat*, based on Anne Rice's *Vampire Chronicles*, with a score by Sir Elton John and Bernie Taupin. Rob frequently directs rock concerts, and has worked with such artists as KISS, Alice Cooper, Dresden Dolls, Cyndi Lauper, and guitar legend Steve Miller. Rob's concert productions have played at the most prestigious venues around the world, including Madison Square Garden, Radio

ABOUT THE AUTHOR

City Musical Hall, Royal Albert Hall, and the LA Forum. *WARHOLCAPOTE* debuted at the American Repertory Theater in a production directed by Michael Mayer. Rob is an avid collector of rock and roll graphics, amassing one of the world's largest collections, which is the subject of the coffee table book *The Art of Classic Rock*. Rob and his husband, Dr. Patrick Meade, live in New York with their yellow Lab, Tag.